AL PURDY

ESSAYS ON HIS WORKS

WRITERS SERIES 9

SERIES EDITORS

ANTONIO D'ALFONSO AND JOSEPH PIVATO

Guernica Editions Inc. acknowledges support of
The Canada Council for the Arts.
Guernica Editions Inc. acknowledges support from
the Ontario Arts Council.
Guernica Editions Inc. acknowledges the financial support of
the Government of Canada through the Book Publishing
Industry Development Program (BPIDP).

AL PURDY

ESSAYS ON HIS WORKS

EDITED BY LINDA ROGERS

GUERNICA

TORONTO·BUFFALO·CHICAGO·LANCASTER (U.K.)

2002

Linda Rogers, Guest Editor
Guernica Editions Inc.
P.O. Box 117, Station P, Toronto (ON), Canada M5S 2S6
2250 Military Road, Tonawanda, N.Y. 14150-6000 U.S.A.

Distributors:
University of Toronto Press Distribution,
5201 Dufferin Street, Toronto, (ON), Canada M3H 5T8
Gazelle Book Services, Falcon House, Queen Square,
Lancaster LA1 1RN U.K.
Independent Publishers Group,
814 N. Franklin Street, Chicago, Il. 60610 U.S.A.

First edition.
Printed in Canada.

Legal Deposit — Third Quarter
National Library of Canada
Library of Congress Catalog Card Number: 2002102768
National Library of Canada Cataloguing in Publication Data
Main entry under title:
Al Purdy : essays on his works
(Writers series ; 9)
ISBN 1-55071-162-8
I. Purdy, Al, 1918-2000 — Criticism and Interpretation.
I. Rogers, Linda. II. Series: Writers series (Toronto, Ont.) ; 9.
PS8531.U8Z56 2002 C811'.54 C2002-900480-2
PR9199.3.P8Z56 2002

CONTENTS

ACKNOWLEDGEMENTS

"Al Purdy's Poetry: Openings" by Stan Dragland was first published in *The Bees at the Invisible: Essays on English-Canadian Writing.*

"Remembering Al Purdy by Susan Musgrave was originally published as a chapbook by Hawthorne.

"32 Uses for Al Purdy's Ashes" by Susan Musgrave first appeared in *Border Crossings.*

"Purdy's Dark Cowboy" by Rosemary Sullivan was first published in *Essays on Caandian Writing: Al Purdy Issue,* No. 49, Summer 1993.

"The Poetry of Al Purdy" by Dennis Lee was first published in *Body Music,* The House of Anansi.

"The Declining Days of Al Purdy" by Catherine Porter was first published in *The National Post,* April 28, 2001.

The dreamweavers pray for holy incandescences in the frisson when warp meets woof. Who is warp and who is woof when the cloth burnishes? Eurithe Purdy knows who she is and what she has done. We are grateful to her and to Rick van Krugel, musician and artist, who gave technical assistance to this project and created a loving design for the gravestone where Al made it very clear he is impatiently waiting for her.

INTRODUCTION

Reaching for the Beaufort

LINDA ROGERS

Some people have it, what they call jungle essence, not so much a peculiar odour (and Al did have that, his person a blend of passion and ink and, in the days before medical prohibition, a top note of beer) as a charismatic presence that changed the air in a room. I remember looking at him, not long before he died on Good Friday, his final antiestablishmentarian act, and thinking, He or They, Whoever, Whatever, threw the mold away when they made him. Al, our dear friend and stubborn adversary was at once himself and a poetic Paul Bunyan, the mythological Canadian of his generation.

The poet loved to talk about "stinct" and extinct. He was "stinct," every inch of him, for as long as he could. He committed acts of poetry to the very end, loving the poems that came in the mail every day, bringing gratitude, respect and even love, the word he wouldn't say. We are still writing to him and we always will because the man standing in front of the dinosaur in Blaise and Barry-Enright Peterson's audacious photograph is now a legend, silenced by cosmic mistake. He never intended to give up poetry.

In "An Oak Hunch: Essay on Purdy," one of those "gift poems" Phil Hall comes up with silver, the perfect Purdy metaphor:

> between the body & language
> a ravine of call and response
> look down the well for the moonshine.

Now Purdy is moon and the well a long way off, but the dialogue goes on.

Al was taller than other people, louder than other people, smarter than other people (except Pierre Trudeau, the only person, I think, who ever intimidated him) and had straighter, finer hair than other people. His couture was The Full Nanaimo (not a good place for couture) and yet he had a kind of elegance. No one else could wear plaid pants, a Harris tweed jacket, off white (bandleader) shoes and a Hawaiian tie and maintain leonine elegance. He was the king of his jungle, from sea to shining sea. Perhaps it was just that he didn't notice himself. He was that obsessed with his world. It might have been that bodacious young poet standing at the back of the room, or a line he'd just heard, or, even better, written himself, or a shivering phrase delivered by a favourite tenor. Al had enthusiasm. That passion gave him a glow that never left him, not even when he was grooming down (a dressing gown with legs) for the big honeymoon in the sky and surrounding himself with books he could grab at the last moment and maybe bargain his way in should his mother's beliefs about the Day of Judgement be right.

There was much to judge. The reverse side of Al's generous enthusiasm was intolerance for anything and anyone that irritated him or got in the way of his hunger for life, information, pleasure, whatever it took to put him on the highway that drove him to the next great poem. That might include someone asking a stupid question, or giving the wrong answer, or a persistent child. The "up close and personal" was never as important to either Al or to his wife Eurithe, who supported him in every way, through every plague and pestilence, as the poetry we now celebrate as national treasure. We all forgave him his many confessed rudenesses because truth and beauty were his standards and his celebrations transcended every transgression.

In a sense, the charisma was part of the beatification process, for, if we have a national Poet, it is Al Purdy. Al's writing is a map of this land. Just as his letters bore the commercial trademark of landmarks across the land: motels, hotels, libraries, writer's retreats, in your dreams a pub, so are his poems the chart of our progress to a culture. There will never be another who smells so cleanly of the rock and grass and sand and dirt that makes this country as unique as Al was as a poet.

This collection is a gathering of friends who appreciate the man and his work with the same objectivity he brought to his many friendships. Literary appreciation is mixed with qualification. As Michael Ondaatje and Dennis Lee remind us, Al was a dreadful poet when he started out. The miracle is that he persevered and made something of himself just as we were building a civilization. His parallel growth with the culture, the self-absorption of the poet and the country as they looked at themselves in the mirror of the twentieth century, is charmingly ingenuous. We are swept away by candour, the large canvas of Al's Canada and inspired to be part of it.

One of those is Catherine Porter, who, on the first anniversary of Al's death, reported in *The National Post* what it meant to the new generation of writers who understand the family connection to him. Her intimacy with the poet was Biblical. Like the prophets of Israel, the First Promised Land, there is a sexual-pedagogical mix in the seeds he has sewn, a frisson she felt in the letters and meetings that made their friendship more than a lesson or a flirtation between an old man and a young woman, something seminal in her life.

Stan Dragland's conversational essay is first in this book because, Eurithe asserts, it was Al's favourite. He liked a no-bullshit kind of guy who knew everything but took pains to tell it like it is, straight up, the way a real man orders a drink in a bar. If you wanted to make Al mad, you just had to make sure someone asked him one of those "clever for their own sake" questions. That really got him going. He cherished his roots, the rootedness of his cultivated voice and the golden epiphanies that lifted the prosaic moments into song. This collection, which has some of his closest friends explaining why it is that Purdy, who alternately enraged and endeared, speaks so clearly to us, attempts to divine the source of that inspiration.

In that clarity, which he defended as "plainsong," is the complex intonation, explicated by Dragland and Dennis Lee, which is partly the result of his decades long apprenticeship to poetry and partly a very good ear. Al, the autodidact, was absolutely intolerant of any kind of pretension, whether it was musical or intellectual, in poetry. If he had a musical correspondent, I would choose Wagner for his exquisite orchestration and melodic line as impossible to sing as it would be to imitate the line that the spider-like Al spun out from his complex brain with long appendages.

Rosemary Sullivan introduces a paradoxical Purdy, the trickster and "duke of dark corners," himself and the dead poet, whose shadow stretched out in front of him. Sam Solecki and Susan Musgrave reveal friendships and influences, sides of the man that are facets of his poetry. Susan's audacious and tender quasi-elegy, written before Al died, at first appalled and then amused the dying poet who told me, when we were choosing the photo for his last book jacket, his ashes should be on the cover. Susan's poem has a presumption of intimacy appropriate to both their characters and a real grief that surprised us all with its power when the poet finally did subside into the ashes that made their way to the graveyard in Ameliasburg, in spite of Susan's suggestions.

A man's reach should exceed his grasp. Al wasn't reaching for heaven. Like Stan Rogers, the Canadian folk singer he so admired, the Beaufort Sea was enough. If there was a heaven, it was the unspoiled country of his birth, and he did his best to explore and record every inch of it from the Prairie to the Tundra and beyond, toward the uncharted, incomprehensible seas of his imagination. Say the names, he exhorted in a great poem, and he did, making a liturgy out of the ordinary places our ancestors staked in the New Jerusalem.

Those names were translated into many languages and they were spoken all over the world, perhaps least appreciated in the country that gave us one of our founding languages. When I was reading in Britain recently, I heard a well-known critic and poet was calling us colonials "those foreign buggers." How Al would have loved that. He never stopped being the anti-establishment, anti-authoritarian, perennial adolescent. His singspeil is a rebuke to artifice, the patina of a dying civilization unwilling to acknowledge its literary offspring. No wonder they feared his amazing grace in the Medieval classrooms at Oxford. No wonder he raged back.

Like the indulged only child he remained, Al tantrumed and crowed. He was all sunshine and storms, his joy unbridled when affection took him to glory. The images that last are those of a stretched child in a proverbial candy store, his arms in the air, conducting a song on a long playing record, or reverently cradling the book he is quoting from memory, something from the vast collection that taught him everything about being human.

We will not see his like again.

AL PURDY'S POETRY: OPENINGS

STAN DRAGLAND

I

I am a part of all that I have met;
Yet experience is an arch wherethro'
Gleams that untravelled world whose margin fades
For ever and for ever when I move.

Tennyson, "Ulysses"

A sort of human magic

When I first heard Al Purdy read "The Dead Poet" I
was amazed. Here was a poem of beauty and great
concentration, obviously a Purdy poem, but with all
of the Purdy self-consciousness, the rough-edged
Purdy persona, refined out of it. I felt I was hearing
not just a gain in technique but something orchestral.
The tight nesting structure of "The Dead Poet" gave
me visions of a new Purdy volume that would somehow ripple out concentrically from that poem. That
didn't happen in *The Stone Bird.* The book opens with
"The Dead Poet," but it's the typical Purdy miscellany. Not that "The Dead Poet" is anomalous; I think
it is a key to reading Purdy, because so much of Purdy

fits snugly into it. So everything that follows here, however unlikely that may sometimes seem, is about "The Dead Poet." Call it Purdy's mythic poem in Northrop Frye's sense: the poem all good poets sooner or later compose in which their poetic essence is so concentrated that the rest of the writing falls into place around it. That is too neat, of course. Aphoristic neatness is part of Frye's rhetoric. Finding a key is not the same as finding a solution, but the key may certainly be a talisman – pure energy – to hold onto while you wrestle with the possibilities it suddenly opens up.

Wrestling with *The Collected Poems,* for instance. Here is another Purdy miscellany, a huge one. "Homer's Poem" and "The Dead Poet" frame the book, but otherwise the progression is chronological. There are no signposts for a reader making his way through these poems and, page by page, never knowing what's going to happen next. Hold on to that key. If this world appears as random as life, it's meant to, not being sponsored by an external creator and meaning-maker. This life is not pre-organized. That opens an opportunity for the reader: to create the book, the books, that *The Collected Poems* contain. Purdy's effort has mostly been bent to making each poem. In fact, negotiating poem after poem through this book, you keep coming on scenes of making. Often you find yourself looking over the shoulder of various witnesses to creation.

Purdy is more and more trying to re-invent the source, to start afresh, in openness and innocence and without arrogance, trying to find the words to shape the spirit that has not one name but many, and those names only to be spoken in words preserving shadows and glints of them. This is romantic; this is religious; this is a quest for "a lost kind of coherence" ("The Darkness" 278) so vigorous and reverent and irreverent and joyful and precise that it doesn't feel in the least nostalgic – though of course it often involves looking back, for meanings resting in the shift of origins already imagined, at records left by other searchers. Looking back to renew the world. Stepping out of scratch, darkness, chaos, into the very first experience. Then and only then, say these poems made out of words, come the words. The voice that most eloquently carries this news is the voice that never did belong to Purdy, the one whose origin is buried in the blood. Dennis Lee's borrowing of the term "tremendum," "meant to honour the mystery, not to straitjacket it" (385), helps to zone the experience of reading Purdy's poetry of the 1980s, those "poems of an extraordinary yet often inscrutable clarity" (387) that Lee opens the way to seeing. Purdy has been courting the inscrutable "deep core of the world" ("The Cartography of Myself," *No Other Country* 17) for decades, and talking about it in poetry and prose, but sometimes, more often recently, the discursive voice has fallen silent and a singing has occurred:

the rare arrival
of something entirely beyond us,

beyond the repeated daily dying,
the singing moment.

("Time Past / Time Now" 318)

What a long way the recent "unsigned" masterpieces are from "Home-Made Beer," which I place at the other distant end of the Purdy Spectrum. "Home-Made Beer" and "The Dead Poet": between them a cosmos, but "The Dead Poet" contains it all.

Keep your ass out of my beer!

We got tired of "Home-Made Beer" at Western when Purdy was writer-in-residence, ten years ago. You'd have thought it *the* Purdy poem, it opened so many readings. "At the Quinte Hotel" ("for I am a sensitive man") was usually not far behind, but it wears a bit better than "Home-Made Beer."

Why that same old poem over and over, Al? Don't you get bored with it? I forget what Al said. Something about breaking the ice, maybe, something about variety; nothing convincing. Al, you've got dozens of other poems could break the ice, if you want it broken. We couldn't figure it out. Al didn't strike us as one of the nervous sort, the kind who create their own formula for surviving public appearances.

I remember a reading a year or so later that was different. More than different; it was electric. Not only because Al seemed really interested in reading the poems for a change, but because of the poems he was reading. "The Dead Poet" is the one that hooked deepest in my memory, but there were others, mint-new poems about beginnings, in the womb, in the garden.

The Stone Bird, with some of the new poems in it, came out in 1981 and I invited Al down to Western for a reading on October 7, 1982. I figured I knew Al well enough by now to throw him a curve in the intro., even though, as introducers go, I'm the nervous sort. So I introduced Al as an established poet whose wonderful new poems were exploring such fascinating new / old territory that he couldn't possibly ever again open a reading with "Home-Made Beer."

Al was on the platform with me, but he didn't seem to be listening. He had to arrange his books, he had to straighten the desk. It's important to get those heavy teacher's desks aligned just so for a reading, and they make a wonderful racket when they slide. The first time Al looked up was when I mentioned "Home-Made Beer."

"Whaddya mean? Ya want me to read 'Home-Made Beer'?"

A Pause. In a cold country you have to deal with frozen water a lot. Sometimes you're breaking the ice; sometimes it's getting thin underneath you. I hate it when that happens in front of an audience.

"You do whatever you like, Al," I said. If this story had a hero, it wouldn't be me.

Mine was the nth introduction to a Purdy reading; maybe Al wasn't paying attention. Maybe he mistook my reference to "Home-Made Beer" for a request.

But it's equally possible that, keeping "an absolutely straight face" (see "Notes on a Fictional Character" 111) Al was saying, "Up yours, Bud." I have never been able to read that occasion; all I know is that for the nth time Al's reading began:

> I was justly annoyed 10 years ago
> in Vancouver . . .

The shape of home is under your fingernails

"I'd prefer to be understood with a minimum of mental strain by people as intelligent or more so than myself," says Purdy in "A Sort of Intro" to *Bursting into Song.* If that were all he wanted, if that was the length of his reach, I doubt that his poetry would be cause for celebration, but it's not an unworthy ambition. Realizing that almost keeps me from saying that "Home-Made Beer" doesn't create any mental strain at all. Well, the reputation is not built on it, not for those who find their Purdy on the page, at least. A lot of the reputation is based on that unmistakeable Purdy voice, though, on the "I" that gets to be "joyfully and relentlessly Al Purdy" in and after *Poems for All the Annettes,* according to George Bowering in his 1970 book on Purdy (21). With the voice comes the image of the sprawling, brawling, beer-drinking, straight-talking impermanent husband familiar to people who have never met Purdy, just as they feel they know Ameliasburg and that "watery omphalos" (Woodcock 9), Roblin Lake. What should be said about that voice and the myth of Al Purdy is that, while neither would exactly be contradicted by having a beer with the guy, they were not somehow transferred whole from the life into the work. The "I" in those poems is the painstaking creation of decades and many false starts; that persona is made of words. If it turns out that behind the persona is an artist who now commands a wide range of styles, the capacity to modulate between a vernacular or "low" style ("Home-Made Beer" would be an instance) and a lyrical high style (as in "The Dead Poet"), there is a sense in which the whole concern, including Purdy's social and political conscience, rests on the vernacular base. Knowing this makes me less impatient when, as in "The Horsemen of Agawa," the base sounds more like interference than a modulation of voice, unnecessarily grounding the lyrical flight.

Some god in ourselves buried deep in the dying flesh

Michael Ondaatje's Caravaggio escapes from the penitentiary outside of Kingston by strapping himself to the roof and letting the other two members of the roof-painting detail paint him, blue on blue, invisible. After dark he unstraps himself and shinnies down.

When Caravaggio got loose, he could have fled in any direction, so what pulled him west, towards Trenton, to cross paths with six year old Alfred Purdy? It must have been Ondaatje's reading of the

memoir, *Morning and it's Summer,* written by the
adult Al Purdy; maybe this passage in it: "Some part
of me still remains a child: sitting on a pile of lumber
behind Reddick's Sash and Door Factory in 1924,
trying to explain to myself how I got here and what
I'm going to do about it" (11). At least it's behind
Reddick's Sash and Door that Caravaggio finds Al,
who scarcely bats an eye when this blue man walks
up. There is a movie currently being shot in Trenton,
which might somehow explain this dramatic colour-
ing, but Al doesn't need an explanation. He is not
much older than the child of "Pre-School" (one of the
autobiographical poems "introduced" by the memoir) who is just discovering primary colours, naming
them and proving to himself "that I could invent the
world" (40). A blue person probably wouldn't stretch
him much.

What kind of gesture is this borrowing of the main
character of *Morning and It's Summer* to play a minor
role in Ondaatje's novel, *In the Skin of a Lion?*
Ondaatje is always "deviously" thinking out plots
"across the character of his friends" ("Burning Hills"
Rat Jelly 56) so the gesture is anything but isolated. It
should be recognized as part of the network of such
references in the discontinuous multi-genre roman a
clef that Ondaatje is writing, but each one raises its
own questions. To judge by the fun it is to recognize
Purdy in Ondaatje's novel, the guest spot is a sort of
friendly joke: Ondaatje hospitably opening his fiction
to another writer's "actual" past. Purdy can't have
expected his character to find a second life beyond

the covers of his memoir, but I doubt that he'd mind. Privately, he might even be pleased to have been offered a compliment in "trickster skin" ("Uswetakei-yawa" *Trick* 91). Of course he would respond in kind. Ondaatje's interest on the loan of young Al was a copy of *In the Skin of a Lion.* The story goes that Al wrote back to say he couldn't find a trace of himself. (The story goes on, in a later instalment: Al got impatient with looking for himself – he'd been warned that he might show up – and wrote to complain about his absence, having given up a couple pages too soon.) If Purdy was pleased, it would probably be because he has said that he feels Ondaatje "writes under the skin." I understand this to mean that you can't catch him at it. He gets under the skin without breaking the surface. Takes one to know one:

> Foregoing the balanced certainty of work,
> And seeking apertures, a loose chink
> In the wall of understanding.
> > ("As a Young Man?" *Pressed on Sand* 13)

In all our bones the long history of becoming

There is a passage in a poem called "Wanting" that catches a doubleness typical of the stance in Purdy's poems, at once inside and outside the experience:

> I bow low over a woman's hand and
> suspiciously glance sideways just in case
> some sonuvabitch is grinning.
> > ("At Marsport Drugstore" 19)

This is actually what it is to be Anglo-Canadian,
inhibited from fully living the moment. We've made
an art of poking fun at the famous Canadian diffidence. Give it a twist, though, and it turns out to have
a shiny side. It's because he feels the drag on taking
himself too seriously that Purdy can voice the strength
of Canadian hesitancy:

> Sometimes it seems that people of nations
> outside my country's boundaries are dancing
> and shouting in the streets for joy
> at their great good fortune in being citizens
> of whatever it is they are citizens of –
> And at other times it seems we are the only
> country in the world whose people
> do not dance in the streets very much
> but sometimes stand looking at each other
> in morning or evening as if to see there
> something about their neighbors
> overlooked by anthropologists
> born of the land itself perhaps
> what is quietly human and will remain so
> when the dancing has ended.

("Home Thoughts" 361)

The quiet reflective rhythms, voice of refined simplicity, this resounding understatement is typically Canadian too, and it is a rock on which something can be
built. It's "a place to stand on" ("Roblin's Mills [II]"
133).

These inner rooms / one cannot enter
   waking . . .

The speaker of "Lament for the Dorsets" witnesses
the last few moments before silence falls on the last
Dorset. Purdy typically names this man and drama-
tises his finale. As a result, watching Kudluk's quiet
death, one feels his race disappear. The puzzled
Kudluk's last act is the carving of a tiny ivory swan.
Meant to speak to a dead person, it is the Dorset's
pivot into the future, because the beauty of the carving still speaks to us.

The swan as proof against death is the image the
poem looks towards and ends with, but I'm more
interested now in another survival, that of Kudluk
himself. He is one of the Dorset giants who "lurk
behind bone rafters / in the brain of modern hunters." This brain which houses ancestors is a metaphor
at the heart of Purdy's perennial preoccupation with
the layers, "all condensed like a compacted millen-
nium" (xv), in the individual mind. A variation on the
metaphor also helps him focus on the mysterious
sources of his poetry. "Where does the song come
from," is the question asked in "The Dead Poet." One
answer is suggested by the image of a Purdy whose
own mind is a muse-occupied dwelling.

There are more Purdy introductions to Purdy
books than one might expect, given that he tends on
those occasions to undermine the value of introductions. To read these is to swing, in prose, through
much of the spectrum of style and approach found in

the poems. At the ballsy end I would place the jokey
hardboiled "Autobiographical Introduction" to the
NCL *Poems* of Al Purdy, and at the poetic end I would
place the rather tender "To See the Shore: A Preface"
to *The Collected Poems* of Al Purdy (not to mention
the lyrical *Morning and It's Summer*). Of course
disarming casualness appears in the serious introductions, and mysteries are mentioned in the more off-
hand ones – like the mystery of that mental warehouse,
and how to get into it.

   "What each of us writes," Purdy says in the "Introduction" to *A Handful of Earth,* "balances and
juggles the whole history of literature, and we are for
that moment the 'midland navel-stone' of earth." But,
he also says, poems "connect with sources I'm not
even aware of, and if I were the poems would be
impossible." In "A Sort of Intro." to *Bursting into
Song* this becomes, "I write because I do not know,
or know very little." Aimed at non-specialist readers,
Purdy's introductions scarcely qualify as poetics. The
casual approach would explain a natural enough al-
ternation between confidence and diffidence on the
subject of the muse. "To See the Shore" may not get
much nearer the truth of what, after all, works only
where it hides, but the image for it, a variation on that
dwelling metaphor and the technique which brought
Kudluk up close, is sustained.

   "Inner recesses of the mind are not at your beck
and call," Purdy says in "To See the Shore."

Perhaps there are small elves in the head, privileged
     guests
living there and continually busy with their own affairs.
The only connection the conscious mind has with them
     is when
they permit a collaboration, which perhaps neither the
conscious nor the unconscious was capable of alone.

                                                            (xvi)

This low-key, un-bardic image of the muse, or muses,
is typical Purdy. "They are very old," he says about
these occupants, "collaborators," custodians of the
wisdom of the ages, quite familiar to readers of
folktales. "You try to predict their thoughts during
the sun by day and the moon by night, then discover
they have their own internal moons and suns" (xvii).
Something fascinating happens here to the image of
the mind as a dwelling. Its walls and roof dissolve to
reveal an alternative interior universe, the key to it
lost or broken. "It's only when I forget about [the
elves] entirely," Purdy says, "that they gently intrude
into my thoughts" (xvii).

    To look for Al Purdy in his poems, and not only
recent ones, is often to find his features, his voice,
re-composed into those of another: someone like
Menelaus, say, telling his heartbreaking story about
Helen, or like an unnamed stone age misfit on the
brink of discovering that he was born to follow
something "into myself to find / outside myself,"
about to discover that he is an artist, though his
existence predates both the term and the role. Sometimes the voice of the poem is all but unrecognizable

as that of the man who wrote "Home-Made Beer."
Such poems seem sung, without mediation, by the old
ones themselves. If Jay Macpherson's Noah, carefully
balancing the golden bubble of his creation-contain-
ing head, had a voice it might sound like this gentle
powerful singing. "Angel declare: what sways when
Noah nods?" is the question of Macpherson's "The
Anagogic Man," and the answer returns: "The sun, the
stars, the figures of the gods" (*Poems Twice Told* 42).

It surprises me to be seeing Purdy clearer by the
light of Jay Macpherson, whose poetry I also love. I
doubt that either poet would be flattered by the
connection. Jay Macpherson's Emblem Books published Purdy's 1962 chapbook, *The Blur in Between*,
but if the two have something mythopoeic in common now it would be because they have written
towards each other from opposite ends of the literary spectrum: the personal and locally particular,
in Purdy's case; in Macpherson's, the literary and
archetypal.

It's not surprising that, in "To See the Shore," (as
in the poem called "Ritual") Purdy endorses Mircea
Eliade's "theories about myth and legend: primitive
peoples re-enact original events in ritual repetitions,
and each time becomes for them the first time. And
thus they negate huge areas of time itself" (xv). For
years now, the Purdy who is deeply rooted in twentieth century Prince Edward County, Ontario, has
been vaulting over centuries, millennia, over the
whole globe and bringing back authentic news of
remote times and places. "In the poetry of the eight-

ies," Dennis Lee says, "there is a greater willingness to speak of first and last things without jokey or belligerent irony, long his defence against sentimentality and pretentiousness" (386). But I come back to singing. I feel that Purdy doesn't speak, so much as he sings, in some of these new poems. He sings, from inside, the very unfolding of birth, the opening of the world.

Purdy gets antsy in the presence of "the high gods of serious things" (xviii), of course. You can find his own version of himself as Noah at the end of "To See the Shore," "aboard a rowboat floating in the middle of all the beer I've drunk in a lifetime" (xviii). He cherishes the subversive in himself, but he knows there are moments when the trickster hears a compelling voice from inside, or maybe from out there (it hardly matters), and simply stands still to listen.

II

I confess I do not believe in time. I like to fold my magic carpet, after use, in such a way as to superimpose one part of the pattern upon another. Let visitors trip. And the highest enjoyment of timelessness – in a landscape selected at random – is when I stand among rare butterflies and their food plants. This is ecstasy, and behind the ecstasy is something else, which is hard to explain. It is like a momentary vacuum into which rushes all that I love. A sense of oneness with sun and stone. A thrill of gratitude to whom it may concern – to the contrapuntal genius of human fate or to tender ghosts humouring a lucky mortal.

Nabokov, *Speak, Memory*

"Our father which art the earth!"

The poem called "Ritual" is a slightly sardonic meditation on surviving a Winnipeg winter – during which all human systems threaten to shut down – with the aid of some brain-warmth from Mircea Eliade who

> in uncanny mnemonics
> remembers the birth of the world
> for me in his books.

(217)

If the reference to Eliade weren't, so to speak, centred by "To See the Shore," one might let it slide. The ironic context of "Ritual" almost buries its importance. But turning from Purdy to Eliade and back gives a sense of déjà vu. As Eliade says, in *The Myth of the Eternal Return,* "any real act [performed by archaic man], i.e. any repetition of an archetypal gesture, suspends duration, abolishes profane time, and participates in mythical time" (36). You can open Purdy almost anywhere and find something connecting with that. Try "The Nurselog," spoken by a fallen tree tenderly holding its thousand-year history in trust for the seedlings nursed by its decay:

> I remember this in a dream
> when we all dreamed
> as if I were an old repeated story
> once told to me that I retell.

(274-5)

"An old repeated story" – it almost seems a single story, the story of creation. Eliade sees everything

folding back into it; Purdy circles back to tell and tell
and – for the sheer joy in it – retell it in shades and
tints of its infinite variety.

> There are moments of such elation
> in a man's life it's like being struck
> alive on the street by the first
> god one meets at an intersection
> whom one must believe in a second
> time after twenty years of atheism
> You press the stomach of your business
> suit flat and stride on into the sunset
> pretending to be serious
> ("The Jackhammer Syndrome" 168)

If you draw a mental line between the great many such
moments recreated in Purdy's poems, you find a good
many of them observing or narrating or dramatising
a variation on some First or other, in his own experience, or that of someone else, or of the world.

But why, or rather how, does he escape the pre-
dicament of modern man, "the terror of history,"
Eliade calls it, a life comprised of unrepeatable moments, one following another, that collect into a finite
span of years, desacralized and meaningless? The
answer is that he doesn't. Whatever magic Purdy can
do with time, one of his great strengths as a poet is
that he is stuck in his own time and place – rooted in
a process, of course, as poems like "Transient" show.
His vernacular voice, "Home-Made Beer" and many
serviceable, often serious, variants issues from the
here and now, and Purdy very often takes the here
and now for his subject and his theme. He has paid

his dues to the present; he knows the sensation that linear existence is absurd. You can feel the black thrill of the abyss often enough in his poems; it yawns under so much of contemporary experience a man would have to be blind not to notice. Purdy does more than that. Feeling it, he uses his powers to make others feel it as well. Hiroshima, South Africa, the poor of Mexico, nuclear waste – a monster of meaninglessness looks out of his poems at times; he is often enough "mind-lost in an immense / garbage heap of yesterday's details" ("D.H. Lawrence at Lake Chapala" 261).

But there is also that inner chamber with its dissolving walls, the compensating vistas that open up anywhere in time. This doesn't cancel time, but it does the next best thing – subdivides it multiply, restoring some of the duration of lost eras, refleshing ghosts. Especially in the sense that Purdy's muses conduct him again and again to scenes of first unfolding, first seeing, he is Eliade's archaic or primitive or mythic man, eternally returning to versions of a cosmogonic moment when chaos coalesced into something. His fascination with endings fits; the ending curls round to a new beginning, and folds back into the integral wholeness of a continued present. Of course Purdy does not accept the traditional first term in this system – the creating god outside of all, containing all and making it mean. For this and other reasons, there is a huge unignorable difference between him and the anonymous cave-painter of Nerja or of the Agawa pictographs he writes about. But it's remarkable how vividly, how plausibly and presently, such figures appear in his poems. His "primitive brain" ("Lost in the Badlands" 291) does draw him, over and over, to create moments of origin "saturated with being" (Eliade 4). He becomes the living paradox Eliade speaks of as a sort of modern primitive, "a modern man with a sensibility less closed to the miracle of life . . ." (77).

It's no wonder Purdy celebrates the core of vitalism in the person and the writing of that other primitive modern, D.H. Lawrence. Lawrence is the iconoclast whom Purdy salutes for

> the glowing question mark he wrote
> after every single one
> of the million names of God?
>
> ("D.H. Lawrence at Lake Chapala" 262)

The sentence is not interrogative, so the question mark is Purdy's way of saying "me too." This independent Lawrence is the one on whose refutation of the New Testament version of creation ("In the beginning was not the Word / – but a Chirrup") Purdy builds one of his loveliest cosmogonic poems ("In the Beginning was the Word"). Lawrence is one of those for whom the dismissal of God and transcendent Elsewhere Reality makes the earthly present throb with value. His reverence for life needs no single source to credit. In an unusual gesture, Purdy gives over the conclusion (the consolation) of his elegy, "Death of DHL," to DHL, making this celebration of the miracle of living his own:

> "For me, the vast marvel is to be
> alive. For man, as for flowers or
> beast and bird, the supreme triumph
> is to be most vividly and perfectly
> alive. Whatever the unborn and the dead
> may know, they cannot know the beauty,
> the marvel of being alive in the flesh.
> The dead may look after the afterwards.
> But the magnificent here and now of
> life in the flesh is ours, and ours alone,
> and ours only for a time.
> I am part of the sun as my eye
> is part of me. That I am part of the earth
> my feet know perfectly, and my blood
> is part of the sea –"

                                                        (324-24)

There is something unPurdy-like in the confidence of this exultation, the centrality in it of the "I," but the faith in the words (such remarkable words to find at the end of Apocalypse, Lawrence's prose commentary on Revelation, and his last book) is near the heart of what Purdy's art is about.

Being Alive is the right title for his collected poems; too bad he'd used it before. Into the wholeness of Lawrence's "here and now," Purdy draws the past, reconciling time and space. It all comes together in the figure of earth, analogous to the teeming brain of the writer, itself a containing brain with a language of its own. "The earth is all things," begins a passage in a poem ("Driving the Spanish Coast") that muses on the significance of the palaeolithic caves at Nerja, Spain, with its "20,000 year-old cave paintings,"

> its shapes greater than imagination
> preconceiving all our discoveries
> all artifacts of man duplicated
> in caves and desert places.
>
> (Stone Bird 45)

Of the many possible openings into the "primitive" Purdy, then, I choose his reverence for earth – stone, in the first place, and a totemic initiation into kinship with stone that happened in the arctic.

The arctic visit is quite famous. It produced *North of Summer* and other poems in which Purdy explores the arctic, with its people, as a highly distinctive "region" of the country. The surest proof that Purdy became something more than a tourist in the north, though, is an experience that was not recorded in *North of Summer*. Purdy puts it this way in "The Cartography of Myself," the essay which opens No Other Country:

> I lay with my ear flat against the monstrous stone
> silence of [Kikastan] island, listening to the deep
> core of the world – silence unending and elemental,
> leaked from a billion-year period before and after the
> season of man.
>
> (17)

"After?" Human existence is parenthesised, a short-lived "season," by the eons of time compacted into this stone that speaks – a silence. The passage is brief, but it obeys some of the stresses in the stone it describes, and it's one of those passages in Purdy one returns to, because he circles back to the experience, renewing it in the title poem of *The Stone Bird*.

This poem is addressed to a woman in pain. She is recoiling from the "terror of horror of being / alive in this sewer world." The obverse of the coin of Lawrence's "marvel of being alive" is a dark reality Purdy never denies, or his essential optimism would carry less force. In "The Stone Bird" he reminds the suffering woman of her own faith (lapsed, but perhaps temporarily) in the way things are, a primitive vision of wholeness, then goes on to share with her his own. Founded on that arctic stone.

> once on an arctic island
> at Kikastan in Cumberland Sound
> in a moment of desolation
> I laid my head flat against the island
> a mountaintop of gneiss and granite
> with ice floes silent nearby
> and heard the heart of the world
> beating
> It was a singing sound
> steady and with no discernible pauses
> a song with only one note
> like some stone bird with such a beautiful voice
> any change of pitch would destroy it.

(Stone Bird 107)

"Earth sound" this is, a heart song that Purdy hears because he believes he does, his primitive self quelling the modern awareness that science could offer a demystified account of his experience. (Reminding me of an aside in Eliade: "If miracles have been so rare since the appearance of Christianity, the blame rests not on Christianity but on Christians" 160.) Reminding me of the speaker of a section of "No Second Spring" (*Stone Bird* 78) "listening" to a voice of reality that, like Purdy, he carries in his head –

> a different one
> whose voice spoke in my head
> and who still had something called sight
> instead of this knowing we have
> whether a thing is round or square
> whether it is good to eat or not
> friendly or unfriendly.)

What is the song of the stone bird? It is "all that beginning earth / singing still," singing all that was and is in time and space.

> those geologic ages
> convulsions of history and pre-history
> all those dawn murders rapes and cruelties
> are condensed into one symphony
> are singing in my ears
> – a wind-song a sun-song
> an earth song and a song of the sea.

"Listen," the poem insists ("listen" is a key word in Purdy; it's the first word of the first poem in the *Collected*), listen to this "song of life"; you can hear it anywhere. Listening is not necessarily a pleasure, since the song is of ill as well as of good, but it all returns to that core of origin, made simultaneous (intelligible) to the ear, if not to the mind.

Perhaps because "The Stone Bird" is a little talky and diffuse it was omitted from the *Collected Poems.*

But it interests me greatly as the record of an actual,
concrete, "historical" experience of return to origins.
It has helped me to notice the many other responses
to "earth power" ("Transvestite" 212) which ripple
through Purdy's poems. (It is not as though he hears
earth's voice for the first time ever in the north,
though that instance sounds freer of the static that
interferes with the song in settled and developed
areas.) The mythic poem in this stone lineage is
"Gondwanaland." It ends with the image of a "Cairn
on an arctic island" that pays homage to the stone
bird, but it's a lament for lost geological unity, the
earth as single land mass which, in theory, broke up
into "stone islands," "stone galleons." In the poem
the history of everything, animal, vegetable and min-
eral is

> riding ships of floating stone
> without meaning or purpose
> for there never was any purpose
> and there never was any meaning –

After the dash, and a stanza break, there is an oblique
leap away from the nihilistic view into the receiving
senses (hearing first) as registers of . . . let's say
meaning, though the word seems too blunt because
the meaning is happening and will not be abstracted
from its performance. This is far from the only Purdy
poem that embodies meaning as fragile, resistant to
the direct approach, to be taken, if at all, by surprise,
and purest when pre-verbal:

Only that one listened to the birds
or saw how the sun coloured the sky
and were thoughtful in quiet moments
Sometimes in these short lives
when our minds drifted off alone
moving in the space vacated by leaves
to allow sunlight to pass thru
at the wind's soft prompting
there was reasonable content
that we were aware of only afterwards
and clapping our hands together like children
we broke the spell.

The second person plural in this poem means that one
is speaking for many, and this happens in other strong
creation poems like "In the Garden" and "In the
Beginning was the Word." It is more usual for Purdy
to imagine his beginnings in singular and particular
terms, but he has more than one string to his fiddle,
and these plurals (like his dramatised personae) are
signs of his escape from a single self. No one who can't
change shape has any claim to being a voice of the
tribe.

As the myth of the eternal return is to the creation,
so is the "monomyth" (Joseph Campbell's term) to
the story of the hero – the same story discernible
through the countless variations of plot and all the
name changes of the hero. In a lower case way this
sort of return is always happening in Purdy's poems.
When he changes shape he never ceases to be himself.
By probing what is most intensely important to him,
he finds out how to understand (and create) the
primitive figures in his poems. For example, traces of

Purdy's connection with arctic stone appear in the
poem called "Meeting" as it follows the first entrance
into the caves of Nerja:

> the earth possessed a womb
> old as earth is old
> cream-coloured smooth stone
> hidden in blood darkness
> with a surrounding network
> of creamy ganglions and nerves
> in which light flickered and danced
> leading away from the glowing centre
> to join the body of the earth.
>
> (Stone Bird 48)

Three entrances are made to this cave in the one
poem: the primary one is that of a persona (whose
"name was Man"), but this is shadowed by Purdy's
own, centuries later, and also by the entry of writing,
which carries from other poems a context for stone.
Once again, though the terms for it are different,
there is a birth, an awakening to a new spiral of
awareness:

> – something awakened inside the man
> as if he had just been born
> and looked at the new world
> outside himself
> with a vast surprise.

Purdy often returns to such pivotal moments, of
ending or (especially) beginning; and these moments
of birth (of world, of consciousness) stack up as
versions of each other, the same and not the same, so
one feels them opening and widening, approaching

anagogy. There are several other poems I might follow on this track, but the obvious step from the poem I've just glanced at is to another (very different) version of the same experience, an earlier (1973) and parallel poem called "In the Caves" that I'd like to linger with.

"Meeting," to isolate one parallel, leaves the man at a point where he has been charged with the magic of stone whose centre he has touched, whose voice spoke inside him, leaving him with an ambiguous "strength/which some would think weakness," "knowledge that could be ignorance." Such "gifts" are also given to the speaker of "In the Caves" (181-184) a young stumblebum, marginal to his primitive community, unvalued even by himself, because he's no good at hunting (see the "inept hunter" / pictographer of "The Horsemen of Agawa" 176). Typically, in the recent hunt for a "grey mountain," a mammoth, that the hunters of his tribe brought down, his spear went astray. In other ways that hunt was not the same experience for him as it was for the others. For them it happened and was over; to him it keeps happening – and in more ways than one. He has no idea why, but the spears that struck the mammoth now strike him, again and again, and repeatedly the mountain's dying shriek escapes his body.

Primitive peoples do not draw lines of demarcation between themselves and the earth, other creatures, the dead. This commonplace of anthropology would suggest that primitives have unity of being without dissociation of sensibility, to borrow phrases from Yeats and Eliot intended to express what moderns desire and do without. Perhaps the lives of, say, the Bushmen are as harmonious as modern anthropologists claim, though it's interesting how smoothly such visions of unity slide into myths of lost Edens. Coherence interests Purdy, but his stories of primitives don't vanish into the archetype of an organic existence. That idea of primitive harmony in group consciousness and activity would be a joke to the misfit of "In the Caves," and the unity that he does feel – identity with the mammoth – is anything but benign. The others have danced and chanted "to the mountain spirit that it might forgive them," and the ritual has drained their culpability into metaphor. They are blissfully limited men, not visceral junctures of blood bone and stone like the misfit. If you are the mammoth and they kill the mammoth, that unity hurts. This man is a flesh-and-blood demonstration of what, besides awe and expectancy, an encounter with mysterium tremendum (holy otherness) means: disorientation, bewilderment, fear. He is undergoing an initiation, a preparation, but the world is so new that no one else, not even the shaman, can explain what's happening. How is he going to find an outlet for the shriek?

By trial and error he finds out what he can do, what he was meant to be. What he discovers reveals that the poem is a portrait of the artist, another of Purdy's self-portraits. First, with a stick, in the earth, and then in "caves at the edge of the higher mountains/where my people fear to come," he scratches the image of that shriek.

> There is something here I must follow
> into myself to find
> outside myself in the mammoth,

he says as he haltingly discovers a pictorial power analogous to the power of words to carry being. But the power of making and the power of comprehending are not, alas, vouchsafed to the same person.

> the shriek flows back into the mammoth
> returning from sky and stars
> finds the cave and its dark entrance
> brushes by where I stand on tip-toes
> to scratch the mountain body on stone
> moves past me into the body itself
> toward a meaning I do not know
> and perhaps should not.

Neither will any interrogation by Purdy of the old ones, his muse-elves, induce them to address him directly. The conduit of the power does not question the power; the brain relaxes and lets the hand write what it will.

By a circuitous route, with many backward loops, we have returned to the question that Purdy worries at in his introductions and in many of his poems ("What it Was" is one of the earliest, 64), realizing that it must be framed as a series of unanswerable questions that nestle one inside each other like Russian dolls: where does the song come from? where does meaning live? and so on. Purdy doesn't write of any single origin, first cause, except to say why the search for such is futile:

> – and if there was anywhere
> a First Cause
> it had hidden itself perfectly
> by remaining in plain sight
> without intention or design.
>
> ("Journey to the Sea" 258)

I doubt that Purdy is interested in a philosophical Primary; it's the sacred spirit source he's after, and he taps it in a large variety of poems that are different and the same. His beginnings are multiple, and they are not points but processes. In the beginning was the earth; in the beginning were the beavers; in the beginning was black; in the beginning was a mountain's shriek; in the beginning was a brother writing words on the wall of a womb: such openings Purdy invents out of a direct primitive feeling of basics like primary colours, sun and moon, the four elements, the senses. His myth-making draws from no authority outside of world in time; it begins at the moment a wave of being begins the motion of a poem. His contribution to dramatising events that must in some sense have happened is to speed them up and particularize them minutely (the first view of the first flower "must have been around 7 A.M." according to "In the Early Cretaceous" 348; the arrival of the "Great Dying" of dinosaurs was the morning after the evening "the sun went down at 5:30 / P.M." in "Lost in the Badlands" 296) and to supply a finely-tuned set of human senses to register them. The authority of these poems is not that of writ, but of the senses; not retrospection but observation.

Originals are not divisible

"The Dead Poet" is tightly woven of the various materials Purdy has used to make his poetry as a whole – conjunctions and disagreements of native and exotic, female and male, life and art. The practical and the poetic, dream and reality, repetition and variation, then and now – in parentheses of first and last things – and it is the right poem to end Purdy's *Collected*. There, isolated by a blank page and italic typeface, it holds Purdy's whole career, near enough, in four shapely stanzas. I sensed this largeness when the poem first thrilled me in 1980 – the active suspension of so many elements, separate words incandescing in the energy of their association.

The scope of this small poem is large, but its intensity is owing to its stress on a single subject, the relationship of the speaker and a fictional dead brother who is projected as an answer to the riddle of the speaker's existence, the reason why, despite his practical pioneering heritage, he should have become a poet. Perhaps the dead brother of this poem has a foundation in reality – a miscarriage, or even the wish of an only child. A dead brother is unurgently referred to in at least two other poems.

But Purdy could never have been as close to a flesh and blood brother as his speaker is to a spirit-brother, maker, who fashioned him, in his own image, a poet. The dead one is the forerunner. Knowing that being alive (we are remembering what this means to Purdy/ Lawrence) is to be denied him, he makes sure that his

brother will live in his place. There is almost a sense
that the one who got born is an impostor, living
moments of greatest intensity in words he does not
own. The dead poet, being family, is a blood version
of those estranged muse/elves. He is the only kindred
spirit in the family at large. The poem's elegiac sadness is for this soul who never lived in the flesh, except
vicariously, and for the poet's loss of a companion
who might have made him less lonely. (See "Night
Summer" 228: "a music / that is complete forgiveness
/ for being" is "not to be known unless the lost self /
aches.") "The Dead Poet" turns A.M. Klein's wonderful "Portrait of the Poet as Landscape" inside out,
since the question it asks is "where do the words come
from?" not "where do they go?"

The last stanza of "The Dead Poet" is a lullaby,
sung to the brother in return for his "faint lullaby/
that sings in my blind heart still." "Sleep," it says, and
"wait," not words addressed to one without a future.
The last stanza is the consolation of the elegy, looking
towards another birth, a waking, as a brother once
again prepares a place into which his brother may be
born.

This mirroring of the first and last stanzas is one
of many teasing near-symmetries in the poem. Of
course, the dead brother's preparation of the womb
is purposeful and shaman-like. He makes the womb
a nest for a poet in a ritual combining three arts that
join in poetry: writing "words on the walls of flesh /
painting a woman inside a woman," whispering his
lullaby-song. The dead brother is related to Purdy's

primitive cave-painters, especially the one whose canvas is a womb of stone. The picture of the brother at his work being so concrete and substantial, one tends to forget that he has only the substance of words. He is a fiction who stands for a mystery that can only be guessed at – so the question at the end of stanza two tells us – the source of the words. He is real and unreal, a living ghost, a ubiquitous absence. Inside and outside! The ritual in the womb must have been to prepare a brother to greet his other self in every experience so moving as to call forth words of poetry. Vastly different though they are, the traces or glimpses or whispers of the dead one in stanza three are not random. The mournfulness of the trim they give to monuments of the soul's magnificence reminds me of another amazing Purdy poem, "Spinning," uncannily written in the exact manner of Canada's least-known important poet, Colleen Thibaudeau. In "Spinning," every loved thing is always whirling away and it's necessary to turn at a desperate rate just to catch a glimpse of them going.

As a whole "The Dead Poet" is more difficult to catch than its simplicity might suggest, and the third stanza is the most elusive. It shifts rapidly from image to image through dislocations of syntax, punctuation and tense, a protean unit attached by a colon to the word "wanderings" and subdivided by dashes signalling remarkable metamorphoses.

> Now on my wanderings:
> at the Alhambra's lyric dazzle

> where the Moors built stone poems
> a wan white face peering out
> – and the shadow in Plato's cave
> remembers the small dead one
> – at Samarkand in pale blue light
> the words came slowly from him
> – I recall the music of blood
> on the Street of the Silversmiths.

This is a Grand Tour conducted at lightning speed and featuring some unusual stops. One of these, Plato's cave, is a metaphor for life lived entirely as in a cave, parallel to and remote from Reality. This cave is found only in *The Republic,* and the Ephesus Street of the Silversmiths appears only (Acts 19:24) in the Bible. Purdy has actually wandered in these realms of gold, as, literally, he visited Spain (The Alhambra) and Russia (Samarkand). There are Samarkand poems in the small volume called Moths in the Iron Curtain. There is a certain sense that the wanderer is meeting versions (different and the same) of images his Canadian past in and out of the womb had prepared him for.

Wherever he goes in stanza four, the poet is reverently visiting works of the imagination, monuments to being; wherever he goes, his dead brother precedes him –always powerless, always dependent on the living voice, but nevertheless a seam running through everything worth seeing and doing. No wonder he is called "spirit of earth" (read "spirit of being") in stanza four.

All of the nesting images in the poem, one thing

inside the other – not only the obvious ones in stanza one, but the citizens in the dim cave, the music in the blood – create a feeling of concealment, and seem to acknowledge the interiority of essence. These are buried things. To reach them you have to peel off a layer – of flesh, of appearance. They are inside the poet's skull, in his bloodstream, living a life of their own just under the skin. The nesting images are ambiguous, though. Concealment and imprisonment are the dark faces of protection and nurturing. And this ambiguous custodianship is performed by a collaboration of the senses. The dead brother opens the poem for rhetorically dramatic reasons, but, as I have said, the second stanza is set in an earlier time, and might be discussed first.

Among the poet's ancestors, the sexes fall into their customary positions in the patriarchal order. The men are active, the women passive, submissive, "meek and mild." Their pioneering is domestic, interior; its emblem is the "cookstove and the kettle boiling." This is an image within the larger image of pioneering in which the women fuel with food the "backwoods wrestlers," their men. Wrestling in the backwoods, perhaps, but more likely wrestling with it. Pioneering was a combat, and these pioneers were victorious – so they thought – in clearing the trees (as lumberjacks), planting the crops (as farmers). The process of domesticating this country is caught in just two words, nouns made active by a verb – "wrestling."

I said that the poet has been plucked from the path

represented by all of this muscular, outward-looking
pioneering, but it's nearer the mark, as the layers of
this poem peel back, to say that he is a poet because
his womb-initiation was androgynous. Inside the female womb a masculine spirit creates the totemic
image of a woman while whispering a motherly lullaby. This complex portrait of Purdy's muse is not of
the male's poet's conventionally female muse, but of
a male strongly marked, perhaps even dominated, by
the feminine. A surprising thing to be saying about
Purdy? One large book that might be assembled from
The Collected Poems is an anthology of male attitudes
to the dance, or battle, of the sexes. But the Purdy I
have been following is a male poet highly responsive
to an other in his nature that is, if not feminine, at
least ambiguous in gender. "Spinning" must originate
somewhere near the feminine end of that continuum.
And "The Dead Poet" feels very reminiscent of the
telescoping poems in Jay Macpherson's *Boatman*. It
was James Reaney who named the "myth of things
within things" (30) that holds *The Boatman* together.
Noah's head contains all of humanity; the ark holds
both Noah and his originary pairs of beasts; at the last
judgement the ark sails back into the eye of God. A
précis hardly does justice to the exercise of emotion
and imagination these poems ask of a reader, but
might suggest why the nesting structure of "The Dead
Poet" would call *The Boatman* to mind when I first
heard it read.

    There is such a gentle vision of the restoration of
unity between all things in the last stanza of "The

Dead Poet" that one might not notice how radically it rewrites traditional eschatology. It's wholly characteristic of Purdy's undermining of the humanistic God and his Word that he forgoes all of the apocalyptic fooferaw of Revelation. That is the western world's most familiar telos, though there are others equally dramatic. Ragnarok – any Norse or Germanic Gotterdammerung – makes great theatre, as long as you aren't in the cast, and none of it is a patch on the nuclear finale we have prepared for ourselves. Sometimes it is hard not to think of ourselves as people of the last days:

> In the darkness is no certitude
> that morning will ever come
> in dawn spreading pink from the east
> is no guarantee that light will follow
> nor that human justice is more than a name
> or the guilty will ever acknowledge guilt
> All these opinions arrived at in years past
> by men whose wisdom consisted of saying things
> they knew might be admired but not practised
> arrived at by others whose wisdom was silence
> And yet I expect the morning
> always I expect the sunlight . . .
>   ("Remembering Hiroshima" 161)

It's not by evasion but with determined faith that writers keep writing in such terrible times. I'm thankful that a writer like Purdy can still authentically imagine a completion to the patterns of things that is not apocalyptic, that foresees a tender evolution, into some new / old Garden state. Purdy's version feels like a correction of T.S. Eliot's "The Hollow Men," with its equally unattractive alternative endings, the bang and the whimper. Purdy's substitutes the whoop and the whisper. But, he says, don't expect the whoop – a sound you might hear in the sort of blast that is a party – just listen; carefully. You'll hear the same sounds you hear now, and they will be totally transformed, everything singing itself and its harmony with every other thing.

Now what's going on? No big deal. The riddle of existence is merely solving itself. Only a Canadian could pull off such affirmation deep in the twentieth century, in quiet words cleaned, as they are uttered, by their very unpretentiousness. And here is another respect in which "The Dead Poet" is at the core of Purdy. It is written in the same key as the poem addressed to the man who thought Canada was no nation, and that poem stands in turn for all those in which Purdy expresses his no-nonsense confidence in the value of rootedness in his own country.

One more thing. The diction and the rhythms of this poem are heightened as part of the tightness of the ensemble. I have spoken of singing. This lyrical Purdy is at the other end of the gamut of sound and substance from the Purdy of "Home-Made Beer" (whose colloquialism and rhetoric of understatement, to be fair, are not completely unlyrical). The sound of "The Dead Poet" carries as much of its sad intensity as the sense. There must have been some temptation to fly this voice, to ride it right away into that other country where the dead poet is at home.

As it is, the voice of the poem is largely his. But, astonishingly, this is a Purdy poem. What makes it so is a certain angular irregularity to the rhythm and, especially, an awkwardness in the last stanza:

> do not expect it to happen
> that great whoop announcing resurrection.

An editing reflex, entranced by the general lift of the music, might "clean" this unit:

> do not expect that great whoop
> announcing resurrection.

But this poem, like all of Purdy's poems, is a product of earth. It must not lift free. The resurrection, such as it is, will happen here. It was easy for Fra Lippo Lippi to see how to improve Raphael's line, impossible for him to reproduce the life in those paintings. Al, I withdraw my objection to "Home-Made Beer." There could be no "Dead Poet" without it.

As the best directions have it, you have to cling to Proteus with arms like the jaws of a pit bull. What a fantastic ride this is, thrashing in tandem through his whole anthology of changes! Some readers lose their hold, but those who hang on through all that torque of transformation, the ones who demonstrate that if necessary this embrace is till death do us part, they say that those ones are granted a wish.

You were perhaps expecting a conclusion to my remarks on Purdy, but his poems keep opening up and swallowing the last word.

> February 5, 2001
> Placenta. The spongy vascular organ, of flattened circular form to which the foetus is attached by the umbilical cord, and by means of which it is nourished in the womb, in all the higher mammals, and which is expelled in parturition, the afterbirth.
>
> (O.E.D.)

What do I know now, so many years after I wrote the essay printed above? I mean what needs to be added. I don't think it needs updating to embrace the poetry written after 1986. I had the acute pleasure of editing *Naked with Summer in Your Mouth* (1994), and much might be said about the amazing explosion of youthful creativity that produced that late volume, but the poems don't differ in kind from those I was concentrating on a few years earlier. No, I just have an embarrassment to confess.

Chuckling over a line in "The Dead Poet" ("I was altered in the placenta") and saying that a woman wouldn't make that mistake, Susan Musgrave made me gulp. Was Purdy mistaken about female anatomy and had I missed that? The alteration is metaphorical, but wouldn't it have to take place in the womb? Looking again at the poem, I see at least that placenta and womb are not necessarily identical there:

> I was altered in the placenta
> by the dead brother before me

who built a place in the womb
knowing I was coming . . .

(Collected Poems 369)

Something in the placental nourishment might account for that alteration, but how would the surviving
brother make his way to the womb through the
placenta? I like to know such things, even if I'm not
going to let a mistake interfere with my love of the
poem.

Is this all I have to add to a deeply-felt essay, now
that Al is gone? Well, why not? I'm reminded of
"Trees at the Arctic Circle," the poem-response to
stunted arctic Ground Willow of a man familiar with
"great Douglas firs" and "tall maples" – first scorn
and then admiration, as it dawns on the speaker what
a triumph it is for a plant to show any vegetation at
all when its roots "must touch permafrost" (85). The
ending is as poignantly human as anything Al wrote,
so human and sentimental as to risk wrecking the
poem:

I have been stupid in a poem
I will not alter the poem
but let the stupidity remain permanent
as the trees are
in a poem
the dwarf trees of Baffin Island.

(85)

Me too, Al: stupid. Well, strictly speaking, that's
inaccurate, though in colloquial speech it's dead on

about how it feels to be ignorant. Ignorant, Al, or else stupid: a permanent condition no matter how hard I think and feel. Here's my hand on it.

NOTES

The section titles are lines from Purdy poems: a sort of human magic: "Method for Calling Up Ghosts" 74; "Keep your ass out of my beer!": "Home-Made Beer" 56; the shape of home is under your fingernails: "Transient" 79; some god in ourselves buried deep in the dying flesh: "My Grandfather's Country (Upper Hastings County)" 148; in all our bones the long history of becoming: "Man Without a Country" 314; those inner rooms/one cannot enter waking . . .": Great Flowers Bar the Roads'" 354; "Our father which art the earth!": "Driving the Spanish Coast (Stone Bird)" 45; originals are not divisible: "The Son of Someone Loved" 340.

WORKS CITED

Bowering, George. *Al Purdy*. Toronto: Copp Clark, 1970.

Eliade, Mircea. *The Myth of the Eternal Return: Cosmos and History*. Princeton, N.J.: Princeton University Press, 1974.

Macpherson, Jay. *Poems Twice Told*. Toronto: Oxford University Press, 1981.

Lawrence, D.H. *Apocalypse and the Writings on Revelation*. Ed. Mark Kalnins. Cambridge: Cambridge University Press, 1980.

Ondaatje, Michael. *Rat Jelly*. Toronto: Coach House, 1973.

—— *There's a Trick With a Knife I'm Learning to Do*. Toronto: McClelland and Stewart, 1978.

——. *In the Skin of a Lion*. Toronto: McClelland and Stewart, 1987.

Purdy, Al. *Pressed on Sand*. Toronto: Ryerson, 1955.

—— *Selected Poems* .(Introduction by George Woodcock). Toronto: McClelland and Stewart, 1972.

—— *The Poems of Al Purdy: A New Canadian Library Selection*. Toronto: McClelland and Stewart, 1976.

—— *A Handful of Earth*. Coatsworth, Ont.: Black Moss, 1977.

—— *At Marsport Drugstore*. (With an appreciation by Charles Bukowski). Sutton West, Ont.: Paget, 1977.

—— *Moths in the Iron Curtain*. (Illustrated by Eurithe Purdy). Sutton West, Ont.: Paget, 1977.

—— *No Other Country*. Toronto: McClelland and Stewart, 1977.

—— *The Stone Bird*. Toronto: McClelland and Stewart, 1981.

—— *Bursting into Song: an Al Purdy Omnibus*. Windsor, Ont.: Black Moss, 1982.

—— *Morning and It's Summer*. Dunvegan, Ont.: Quadrant, 1983.

—— *Piling Blood*. Toronto: McClelland and Stewart, 1984.

—— *The Collected Poems of Al Purdy*. Ed. Russell Brown. (Afterword by Dennis Lee). Toronto: McClelland and Stewart, 1986.

Reaney, James. "The "Third Eye: Jay Macpherson's *The Boatman*." Canadian Literature 3 (Winter 1960), 23-34.

THE COLLECTED POEMS OF AL PURDY

MICHAEL ONDAATJE

We were very young and he was hitting his stride –
Poems for all the Annettes, The Cariboo Horses. There
had been no poetry like it yet in this country. Souster
and Acorn were similar, had prepared the way, but
there was a voice with a "strolling" not "dancing" gait
or metre, climbing over old fences in Cashel township
. . . (and who ever wrote about "township lines" in
poems before Al did?)

And with this art of walking he covered greater
distances, more haphazardly, and with more intri-
cacy. Cashel and Ameliasburg and Elzevir and
Weslemkoon are names we can now put on a literary
map alongside the Mississippi and The Strand. For a
person of my generation, Al Purdy's poems mapped
and named the landscape of Ontario, just as Leonard
Cohen did with Montreal and its surroundings in *The
Favourite Game.*

We were in our twenties (and I speak for my
friends Tom Marshall and David Helwig, who were
there with me) and we didn't have a single book to
our names; we were studying and teaching at the
University in Kingston.

. . . And Al and Eurithe simply invited us in. And why? Because we were poets! Not well known writers or newspaper celebrities. Did Kipling ever do that?

Did D.H.Lawrence? Malcolm Lowry had done that for "Al-something or other" in Dollarton, years earlier.

These visits became essential to our lives. We weren't there for gossip, certainly not to discuss royalties and publishers. We were there to talk about poetry. Read poems aloud. Argue over them. Complain about prosody. We were there to listen to a recording he had of "The Bonnie Earl of Murray." And sometimes we saw Al's growing collection of signed books by other Canadian poets (my favourite dedication among them was "To awful Al from Perfect Peggy.")

All this changed our lives. It allowed us to take poetry seriously. This happened with and to numerous other young poets all over the country, right until the last days of Al Purdy's life. He wasn't just a "sensitive" man, he was a generous man.

Most of all we should celebrate his fervent, dogmatic desire to write poetry. A glass-blower makes money. A worm-picker has a more steady income. Al, a man who had the looks and manner of a brawler, wanted to be a poet. And what is great is that he was a bad poet for a long time and that didn't stop him. That's where the heroism comes in.

And when he became a good, and then a great poet, he never forgot the significance and importance of those bad poets – they were rather like those small homes and farms north of Belleville, a little adjacent to where the world is," and about to sink into the earth. He had been there. It gave his work a central core of humbleness, strange word for Al. It resulted in the double take in his work, the point where he corrects himself.

"I have been stupid in a poem . . . "

As he was not ashamed to whisper in a poem-this in a time of mid-century bards. Al never came with bardic trappings.

"Who is he like?" you ask yourself. And in Canada there is no one.

I can't think of a single parallel in English literature. It almost seems a joke to attempt that. He was this self-taught poet from up the road. What a brave wonder.

So how do we respond to all that Al was and stood for?

The great Scottish poet Hugh MacDiarmid, who was pretty close to Al in some ways, had by the time of his death become the embodiment of what his country's culture was, and stood for, and stood against. Fellow Scottish poet Norman MacCaig recognized MacDiarmid's contribution by saying: "Because of his death, this country should observe two moments of pandemonium."

PURDY'S DARK COWBOY

ROSEMARY SULLIVAN

Thinking about a celebration of Al Purdy has been for me an egocentric exercise because it sent me back on a tour of my own history as a reader of poetry. I've had to cope with a number of addictions over the years: it began, as it often does, when I was in my early teens and had my first romance with Wordsworth; and then there was Rilke on one side and Roethke on the other; there was T.S. Eliot and Elizabeth Bishop; there was Yeats; and then there was Al Purdy. There was P.K. Page, Margaret Avison, and, later, all the new contemporary women beginning with Atwood, but then there was Purdy. He always seemed a kind of trickster, a teaser. What was he up to in my mind?

I knew he was a man's poet, he and Lautréamont competing in metaphors: "the sun was a ball of spit on the barroom floor" (a line I recall from Lautréamont); "lost in the dry grass / golden oranges of dung" (Purdy, "The Cariboo Horses," *Collected Poems* 42). Still, Purdy stuck, and it took me a long time to locate the centre he had hit. I realize now I had found in his poetry a magic I was looking for: something to do with memory and place, the essential catalysts of poetry. Place. I had long bought Charles

Olson's notion that localism alone can give rise to culture, but when I started I was puzzled about where I was going to find a path to that localism since my place was Canada – which was, in the 1960s, still ambiguous, self-effacing, self-apologetic, and colonial.

But Purdy found it for me in 1965 in "The Country North of Belleville":

> Yet this is the country of defeat
> where Sisyphus rolls a big stone
> year after year up the ancient hills
> picnicking glaciers have left strewn
>   with centuries' rubble
>   backbreaking days
>   in the sun and rain
>
> When realization seeps slow in the mind
> without grandeur or self-deception in
>   noble struggle
>   of being a fool –
>
>   (*Collected Poems* 61)

I love that poem. But why do I find it so peculiarly comforting? "Without grandeur or self-deception in/ noble struggle / of being a fool." It strikes the essential Purdy note, it reveals his quintessential gaze. It enacts that ironic deflation that prevents you from taking yourself too seriously as you get on with the bizarre business of being human. As Margaret Atwood would say of being human, "does anyone ever achieve it?" (26). As a writer, can you stumble on the clue to the national psyche? Can you affirm for other people their psychic space? Northrop Frye would say yes,

literature is the locus where cultural archetypes surface. And Virginia Woolf writes: "For masterpieces
are not single and solitary births; they are the out-
come of many years of thinking in common, of thinking by the body of the people, so that the experience
of the mass is behind the single voice" (98). Purdy hits
a resonance for me that seems to pull many voices
along with it: "in / noble struggle / of being a fool" –
it's an irony I recognize at the core of Purdy, an irony
that is imaginatively predisposed to dialectic, to bi-
nary oppositions that are held in tension, polarities
that balance. He has the impulse to mediate and
sustain oppositions, not to resolve them. That is
Purdy's dignity. And the reason for my comfort with
his stance may be that, perhaps, it is also a peculiarly
Canadian one.

Al Purdy is a Canadian cowboy, a man from a
Cariboo country he invented in his head, but he's the
kind of cowboy I like. I was at a conference at the
University of Alberta in 1978 called "Crossing Fron-
tiers." Robert Kroetsch was there. Kroetsch was talking about the difference between American and
Canadian cowboys. The Canadian cowboy, he said,
like his American cousin, heads out for the territory
ahead, leaving Aunt Sally in the dust of his horse's
hoofs. But then he begins to doubt. He has second
thoughts. He stops. He circles the house. He gets
caught within the tension between horse/house.
Purdy is always caught on a double hook. He believes
you must sustain either/or. And I think that's what I
like about him. He writes the "Song of the Imperma-

nent Husband." An autodidact, he hides his learning.
"Song" must be one of the few love poems that finds
its erotic authority in Kierkegaard:

> Oh I would
> I would in a minute
> if the cusswords and bitter anger couldn't –
> if the either/or quarrel didn't –
> . . . .
> And you you
>   bitch no irritating
> questions re love and permanence only
>   an unrolling lifetime here
> between your rocking thighs
>
>   and the semblance of motion
>   (*Collected Poems* 45-47)

Permanence in reinvention . . . is that the clue to
Purdy's poetic promiscuity? For his lust for the poem
seems unconquerable, as the range of his *Collected
Poems* makes clear.

He keeps turning back on himself and asking,
"where does the song come from?" At least that's
what he did in 1981 in one of his greatest poems:
"The Dead Poet" (*Collected Poems* 369). And he finds
it comes from the double in the self, the one whose
script he read on the womb walls before he entered
this puzzle of a life:

> I was altered in the placenta
> by the dead brother before me
> who built a place in the womb
> knowing I was coming:
> he wrote words on the walls of flesh
> painting a woman inside a woman

whispering a faint lullaby
that sings in my blind heart still.

(369)

And here is another clue to Purdy. It has always
fascinated me that Robertson Davies has insisted
Canadians are more attached to Jung than to Freud
because "We're great withholders" (37). Purdy is a
Jungian cowboy, a fantastical duke of dark corners.
Behind his up-front persona, the poet with his shoes
covered in "golden oranges of dung," is the poet
obsessed with the darker mystery of memory. If you
want to find the poet in the persona, the man in the
poet, go to his 1983 book, *Morning and It's Summer*.
There you find the poet in reflection, reading the
script on the womb walls:

> There is perhaps something to be said for the idea that
> the best parts of life are the exaltations, those times
> when something happens which so moves one emo-
> tionally that everything else is driven into the far back-
> ground of the mind. The rare occasions when you
> meet "a woman with such a glow / it makes her back-
> ground vanish." Or even the tremendous grief one
> feels at six or seven years old in sympathy for a corre-
> sponding grief and shame in the mind of Jack Corson
> when he was accused of stealing. A sympathy that must
> be so akin to the original feeling that it becomes one
> of the absolutes, like hate, terror and love. For we are
> partial beings in what we feel much of the time, sel-
> dom carried away or captured by one of the unadulter-
> ated emotions, the absolutes, merely nibbled at by
> terror, hate and love. It's likely, of course, that the
> human psyche is too frail, too cobweb fragile to sur-
> vive the full strength of a complete obsession. Fever

would rage through our bodies, fire would spring from
our mouths and eyes.

(26-27)

If we are partial beings, then the only way the poet
has to sabotage that partiality is to become a mythog-
rapher, inventing himself. In Purdy's first myth, he is
the changeling, the child surreptitiously or uninten-
tionally substituted for another, spoken to from
pretime by that other who waits for him back at the
beginning. He needs this myth to explain his sense of
difference, of displacement, of childhood loneliness,
which may always be an essential psychic factor that
poets share in the process of their making: "At that
early time of my life, five, six, and seven years old, I
still had the feeling of belonging somewhere else,
having lately arrived without any explanations given"
(II). The childhood Purdy selects from the debris of
memory is fantastical. I say "selects," but this is not a
deliberate process: it may be that the memories that
lie in the pools of our minds are what, cumulatively,
create us, rather than we them. Purdy seems to say
this:

> Everything small and of little importance: the apple
> blossoms, three black snakes under a fallen door,
> Grandfather and myself, a few trivial moments in the
> 1920s, they were all gathered together at exactly the
> right time for memory to hold them in a synchroniza-
> tion of little separate etchings and images beyond
> time.

(23)

The images he accumulates in his memoir to invent

the man, Al Purdy, are tender. We encounter a Lilliputian boy in a world of aged giants. A boy who believes "God [is] fear," and who is "scared to death of Him" (20). Who crawls over wrecked automobiles and battered fenders twisted into hazardous grating mountains in Merker's junkyard to jig out the pulp books from among the bales of old newspapers, learning early that reading is dangerous. Who lives next door to Campbell's Tombstone Works, where every day but Sunday chisels pound at friendly stone, and the dead never come because they can't stand the noise. Who, though dubious about the actual existence of Santa Claus, sets a trap for him of cunningly concealed threads looped across doorways. And who read the Bible cover to cover: "Jeremiah begat, Joseph begat, everybody begat . . . That was forbidden, that was attractive" (20).

If you ask Purdy outright to give you something of himself, he will stumble and most likely offer you Purdy "At the Quinte Hotel":

> I am drinking
> I am drinking beer with yellow flowers
> in underground sunlight
> and you can see that I am a sensitive man
> > (*Collected Poems* 109)

Or you'll possibly find him sequestered in some Arctic outhouse. It's the trickster's tactic to puncture piety and get a laugh in the bargain. But somehow I always head for the dark corners in Purdy. I like to think of Purdy as a shape shifter, a Proteus. You have to get

him at a vulnerable moment when he's crawled onto
the beach for a rest. He'll squirm and shift into as
many preposterous shapes as he can imagine. He'll
declaim and disclaim, he'll drink you under the table.
But if you hold on you'll find that beneath the raucous
humour lurks that duke of dark corners.

WORKS CITED

Atwood, Margaret. "Margaret Atwood." With Graeme Gibson.
    Eleven Canadian Novelists. Toronto: Anansi, 1972. 1-31.

Davies, Robertson. Robertson Davies: "The Bizarre and Passion-
    ate Life of the Canadian People." With Donald Cameron.
    Conversations with Canadian Novelists. Ed. Cameron.
    Toronto: Macmillan, 1973. 30-48.

Purdy, Al. *The Collected Poems of Al Purdy.* Ed. Russell Brown
    Toronto: McClelland, 1986.

——— *Morning and It's Summer: A Memoir.* Dunvegan, ON: Quad-
    rant, 1983.

Woolf, Virginia. *A Room of One's Own.* London: Hogarth, 1929.

THE POETRY OF AL PURDY

DENNIS LEE

In 1944, at a cost of $200, Al Purdy engaged a printer in Vancouver to produce 500 copies of *The Enchanted Echo,* his first collection of verse. The author was less of an ethereal sprite than the title might imply, being lanky and rawboned in appearance, shambling and somewhat ornery in manner. His debut did not attract widespread attention.

Purdy hailed from United Empire Loyalist country, the region of small towns and rolling farmland at the eastern end of Lake Ontario, where his forebears had settled in the 1780s. He was born there in 1918; his father, a farmer, died two years later. The son grew up in Trenton, in the care of his rigidly religious mother, and left school without completing grade ten. After drifting through occasional jobs, he joined the air force in 1940, and was now stationed in British Columbia for the duration of the war.

A less likely bard-in-the-making would be hard to imagine. And the fact is, Purdy would prove to be among the slowest of developers in the history of poetry. For decades his progress consisted of false starts and apparently unproductive slogging. Only in retrospect can we discern the sureness of instinct which propelled him through his long apprenticeship, till he emerged as one of the fine poets of our time.

1. The Long Apprenticeship

Purdy had been writing verse since the age of thirteen, but in complete isolation from the central developments of twentieth-century writing. The modern poets he knew were those in his school anthologies: Kipling and Chesterton and Turner, Carman and Roberts and Pratt. And the poetry he wrote till he was past thirty is exemplified by the title piece from his book:

> I saw the milkweed float away,
> To curtsy, climb and hover,
> And seek among the crowded hills
> Another warmer lover.
>
> Across the autumn flushing streams,
> Adown the misty valleys,
> Atop the skyline's sharp redoubts
> Aswarm with colored alleys –
>
> I caught an echo in my hands,
> With pollen mixed for leaven –
> I gave it half my song to hold,
> And sent it back to heaven.
>
> Now oft, anon, as in a dream,
> O'er sculptured heights ascending,
> I hear a song – my song, but now,
> It has another ending.

With no other models available, this is where Purdy began. Why he didn't heed the advice he must have had in abundance – to find a job with a future, and stick to writing as a hobby – is beyond ordinary comprehension.

After the war Purdy found himself in Vancouver once more, where he worked in a mattress factory from 1950 to 1955. Then it was back east to Montreal for two years, to the fertile and combative milieu that included Irving Layton, Louis Dudek, Frank Scott and Milton Acorn – Purdy by now having resolved to make himself into a great poet. In 1957 he and his wife built a small house on Roblin Lake, south of Trenton. And there, with no cash, they settled in: Eurithe to earn their keep, he to write. Albeit with an acute sense that he had made nothing of his life so far, that perhaps he was a permanent failure.

In 1960, to pause here at Roblin Lake, Purdy was forty-two. He was reading omnivorously, and since 1955 he had published three chapbooks. He'd out-grown *The Enchanted Echo*. But he still had not produced more than a handful of poems worth keeping.

Some of the reasons for his slowness must lie in the inscrutable private rhythms of any writer's development. But from the vantage of twenty-five years later, it is hard to resist the conclusion that he was trying, however obscurely, to reinvent modern poetry on his own terms. About 1952 he had been goaded by a friend into reading the classics, particularly the moderns. The effect was drastic. Consciously or not, he'd had to accept that the formal tradition was bankrupt, at least for his own imagination. Rhyme, metrical rhythm, fixed stanza forms, and the stock poetical attitudes that Purdy had been parading – these were drawn from a literary universe in which the rough-hewn autodidact from Trenton could never be more than an outsider. If he wanted to become his own large clumsy aching generous eloquent awestricken self in words, he would have to set aside the whole of traditional poetry, start back at square one. In his mid-thirties, he would have to recommence his apprenticeship in earnest.

And at that point, an apparently perverse spirit of independence had taken hold. He would not put himself to school with the great modern masters: not Yeats or Eliot, not Pound or Williams. Nor would he settle into one of the newer styles, with Auden or Dylan Thomas. For better or worse he would negotiate an independent passage – from the weird time warp of (say) 1910, where he'd been stuck, to his own here and now. But there was a price to pay for this stubbornness. Already a late developer, he would now have to spend another full decade catching up with himself.

Mind you, he did gain some momentum by wrestling with other poets. In the mid-1950s he wrote like Dylan Thomas for a year or two. And around 1958, he tried out Irving Layton's verbal flamboyance and self-assertive stance. But the results were more compacted and stiff-jointed than what he was reaching for, and soon he was pressing ahead again. What he needed was a way of writing that fitted him like a skin; that let him enact his own way of inhabiting the world, speak its native inflections. What his hands could touch, what his nerve ends knew – these would be the final test of words. Along with his inner ear.

A clear marker in the transition is the lively but exasperating "Gilgamesh and Friend," from 1959:

> Eabani, or Enkidu, made by an itinerant goddess
> From clay, hairy, perhaps human,
> Destined to have carbuncles, goiter, fear of death –
>
> Became friend of beasts, notable in that
> He learned their language (played the flute?),
> Was weaned from animals by a courtesan. . .
> (How?) Joined Gilgamesh to initiate heroism
> (First known ism?) in the Sumerian microcosm.
> Killed bulls, wizards, monsters like Shumbaba
>
> (Who had no genitals, thanks goodness!) in a cedar
>   forest . . .

By now Purdy has started to loosen up. And the play of energy in the speaker's consciousness is the pent-up something that had been trying, all along, to find its way into his poetry. Letting that energy invade the process of composition – so that the poet simultaneously sketches his subject (like a musical theme) and embroiders it with fancy honks and playful suppositions (like a series of improvised variations) – this looks like the next step Purdy had to take . . . Except it isn't working yet. The set stanza form just gets in the way, a residue of alien convention. And the ostensible subject, Gilgamesh and friend, disappears beneath the avalanche of wisecracks.

By 1960, dug in at Roblin Lake, Purdy was finally in motion. But it still wasn't clear that he was going anywhere of poetic interest.

What happened during the next two years was an abrupt quantum leap, of the sort that defies explanation whenever it occurs. In his collection of 1962, *Poems for All the Annettes,* there are still misfires. But in the best poems, the mature Purdy simply vaults free of three decades of marking time, in a riot of exuberant, full-throated energy.

Now the closed forms of the past are spronged open with a vengeance, releasing a headlong, sometimes dizzying cascade. As in "Archaeology of Snow," where the line breaks and phrasing seem configured by the play of unpredictable energy, rather than being poured into a pre-existing mould:

            Bawdy tale at first
                                what happened
        in the snow
        what happens
                in bed or anywhere I said
                                        oh Anna
                here –
                        here –
        here –
                here –
                        here –

Once having discovered this degree of freedom, Purdy would settle into a more restrained use of multiple margins and spray-gun layout. But claiming such plasticity in the way a poem lands on the page seems to have been a necessary part of the break-through to his own voice.

And the pace of a poem is something he can control with virtuosity. Now certain line breaks occur after a word like "and" or "the" (dragging the reader on to the next line, to complete the unit of thought), while others coincide with a natural pause (recreating the breathers the imagination takes as it finds its way ahead). A canny modulation between these two kinds of line break was another sign of his maturing craft.

The poem has become an act of discovery for Purdy, rather than a list of things discovered. It's full of particulars. And it is fluid, constantly in process; often the lid is not quite banged shut at the end. Now he can catch a wide range of tonalities, from a head-long clatter to a delicate, murmuring equipoise: "Briefly briefly all things / make the sounds / that are theirs – " Or to the grave, almost liturgical hush of "Remains of an Indian Village":

> Standing knee-deep in the joined earth
> of their weightless bones,
> in the archaeological sunlight,
> the trembling voltage of summer,
> in the sunken reservoirs of rain,
> standing waist-deep in the cris-cross
> rivers of shadows,

in the village of nightfall,
the hunters silent and women
bending over dark fires,
I hear their broken consonants . . .

At forty-four, Purdy had come into his own – with all
sirens going. The long apprenticeship was over. He
had found his way to an open poetry which could be
brash, adventurous, tender, self-mocking, sublime;
within which he could move in any direction with
gusto and abandon.

He had made the same journey, from a closed to
an open poetic universe, that other, major talents
have accomplished in this century. But he'd done it
in characteristically maverick fashion. He had refused
to read Whitman, Pound, or Williams, whose free
rhythms and vernacular diction would have made
them obvious mentors. And he'd made temporary
stopovers with Thomas and Layton, who were not
pointing in the direction he would take at all. (D. H.
Lawrence's poetry would soon become a touchstone
for him – but only after 1965, when his own forma-
tion was complete.)

Purdy had found an independent path, to an
unmarked destination, essentially by himself. And in
the process he had become a genuine original.

In *The Cariboo Horses*, three years later, Purdy con-
solidated everything he had learned in the earlier leap
and carried it further. There is now a wonderful
sure-footedness in the rangy, loping gait which had

become his signature – with its ability to open out into vast perspectives of space and time, then narrow down to a single moment or image. It was with this volume that he reached a wide critical and popular audience. And the spate of good and great poems began which have taken on normative status in our literature.

One advance was a new assurance in identifying his subject matter. For years I thought of *Cariboo Horses* as the book in which Purdy claimed his Canadian themes – perhaps because it includes "The Country North of Belleville," one of his first unequivocal masterpieces. But what's starting, on returning to the book, is how much of Purdy's home ground it claims. Here are the portraits, the vignettes, the early memories, poems of place, jokey breakneck yarns, on-the-spot reportage, har-de-har asides, delicate evocations of love and the natural world, broad satire, distant times and places: sex and death and poetry, the galaxy and Roblin Lake.

Above all, it's the book with the magisterial authority of lines like these:

Old fences drift vaguely among the trees
        a pile of moss-covered stones
gathered for some ghost purpose
has lost meaning under the meaningless sky
        – they are like cities under water
and the undulating green waves of time
        are laid on them . . .
                ("The Country North of Belleville")

With the appearance of *The Cariboo Horses*, in

Purdy's forty-seventh year, this story of late-bloom-
ing, interminable, and heroic apprenticeship comes
to completion. We need a different approach than the
chronological to take the measure of the next three
decades.

2. The Process

Surveying Purdy's mature poetry as a single body of
work, stretching from 1962 to the present, reveals
some large recurring features. One is the vision of
process which informs his poetry. (I'll let the term
gather its meaning as we proceed.) This vision is first
of all historical. It's conceivable that growing up in
Loyalist country (albeit with no great family stress on
tradition) contributed to Purdy's sense of organic
continuity in time. Certainly he has written often and
well about the persistence of the past in that milieu.
"Father and grandfathers are here," he says, "grand-
mothers and mother / farmers and horsebreakers /
tangled in my flesh / who built my strength for a
journey" ("In the Dream of Myself"). And in the two
poems entitled "Roblin's Mills" he concentrates so
hard on the nineteenth-century inhabitants of his
town that he is granted contact with their lives, and
communes with their "departures and morning ru-
mours / gestures and almost touchings." Though they
must subside again into the past, their continuity can
now be gravely affirmed: "they had their being once
/ and left a place to stand on."

Even when the legacy of the past is indecipher-
able, that very message of obliterated purpose tells
Purdy something about his roots. In "The Country
North of Belleville," he meditates on inscrutable
stone-piles and fences that no longer enclose anything, their farms long abandoned. And the choric
lament rises in him: "This is the country of our
defeat." Both the strength and the failures of the past
live on in time.

For Purdy, time is a continuum that permits a com-
merce of dead with living, of living with dead – rather
than being a wasteland, say, or an executioner. And
so his sense of time passing is bittersweet, rather than
merely bitter.

On the one hand, he laments what perishes. In
"Elegy for a Grandfather," he expands on the old
man's death to mourn for everything that dies:

> and earth takes him as it takes more beautiful things:
> populations of whole countries,
> museums and works of art,
> and women with such a glow
> it makes their background vanish
>   they vanish too,
> and Lesbos' singer in her sunny islands
> stopped when the sun went down –

Yet on the other hand, things don't just die. Thus he
can remark (in "Temporizing in the Eternal City") on
how "the past turned inside out / protrudes slightly
into the present." Such continuity in time may not
remove the scandal of transience and death, but it

qualifies them in a nourishing way. Looking at the sculpture of Beatrice, he observes "something crouching there / joining the cadences of eternity."

So far, Purdy can be seen as having a sense of the partnership of human beings through time – as indeed he does. But to stop there would be to miss everything weird, wonderful and distinct in his vision of space-time as a process.

We can glimpse this vision as early as "Night Song for a Woman" (perhaps his first fully mature poem, written in 1958). It's a mysterious little piece, truly a night song.

> A few times only, then away,
> leaving absence akin to presence
> in the changed look of
> buildings
>   an inch off centre –
>
> All things enter
> into me so softly I am
> aware of them
>   not myself
>
> the mind is sensuous
>   as the body
>   I am a sound
> out of hearing past
> Arcturus
>   still moving outward
>
> – if anyone were to listen
> they'd know
>   about humans.

Something has happened to Purdy "a few times only, then away" – but what is it? The poem doesn't appear to say, though perhaps "All things enter into me" gestures at an answer. Again, how does Purdy suddenly find himself on this extraordinary jaunt out past Arcturus? And what is it that people would "know about humans" if they listened? Finally, on a very different tack: what enables these disconnected snatches to hang together at all? Palpably they do, in a breathless murmuring which seems suspended in eerie silence. But what is the source of their coherence?

We won't try to answer these questions yet. But it's evident that the universe according to Purdy operates on unfamiliar principles. It is not just that he can suddenly mutate into "a sound / out of hearing past / Arcturus / still moving outward" – but that the phenomenon is taken so for granted slipping across the galaxy is as much a matter of course as slipping across the street. And once we recognize that, we can see that the same thing keeps happening – with all sorts of variations – throughout the whole of Purdy's work. Take a step in any direction and you find yourself in the nineteenth century, in long-ago Samarkand, in the Upper Cretaceous or outer space. The cosmos of Purdy's poetry is one in which familiar laws of movement in both space and time may be suspended without warning, and a different set of principles take over. A second or alternate universe is latent in the familiar one, and can assert itself at any time. What's intriguing is to chart the behaviour of this parallel reality – the cosmos of process.

In "Hockey Players," a game is suddenly detonated
when three players swerve out of quotidian space, and
into the alternate cosmos. They end up "skating thru
the smoky end boards out / of sight and climbing up
the appalachian highlands / and racing breast to breast
across laurentian barrens" In itself, the moment is
fanciful but the underlying experience – of swerving
out of the conventional world, and then covering
ground so quickly that space collapses into a blur of
simultaneity – is pure Purdy.

In *The Cariboo Horses:* he watches cowboys riding into 100 Mile House on their "half-tame bronco
rebels." He resists the impulse to romanticize the
horses; yet even as he does he finds himself carried
elsewhere and elsewhen, transfigured in contemplation of "the ghosts of horses battering thru the wind
/ whose names were the winds' common usage /
whose life was the sun's." Only at the end of the poem
does he return to the scene before him. It's a remarkable affirmation of parallel universes – of a day-to-day
world, and a larger, more luminous one. And in the
alternate universe, points far separated in space and
time are simultaneous.

Again, standing "At the Athenian Market" Purdy
moves into a kind of lucid trance. Now a pile of
oranges is "involved with converging lines / of light
Phidias the sculptor / laboured over half an hour /
ago." And as the sight of the living girls in the
marketplace carries him deeper into trance, he moves
to union with "long ago girls" – and then, unexpectedly, further back still, to the first emergence of life

from primordial waters, and to the very beginnings of evolution, "before these Greek cities / before the sea was named / before us all." Yet in truth Purdy doesn't even seem to be "moving back"; this is a stillness which goes beyond the wild canter of "The Hockey Players," and participates in other points in space-time with out stirring an inch.

The poem is characteristic in that it sounds the note of lived, authentic exaltation precisely as it enters the aspect which seems the most remote from "real life" – that is, the intuition that all time and space are simultaneous. It's at this juncture that Purdy's poetry regularly takes on the nostril-flare or hush, and the quirky, kindled gait and diction, which make it irreplaceable – and which feel utterly unforced, at home in a mystery they know firsthand, "as the days and nights join hands / when everything becomes one thing" ("The Dead Poet"). The intuition feels more real than mundane reality.

The distant past juts into the immediate present; far away is near at hand. Space-time is plastic, elastic, fantastic. We don't yet know what that signifies. But there are examples by the hundred in Purdy's work; start reading with this in mind and it crops up everywhere, this "simultaneity of things / . . . the instant of the dinosaurs / whose instant I am part of" ("Lost in the Badlands"). The cosmos of process is close to being the primary universe of his poetry.

I have been speaking of Purdy's parallel cosmos, and

referring to it as one of process. So far, the meaning
of "process" seems to be mainly that a great deal of
high-speed traffic goes on in the space-time continuum.

But there is more to it than that. For it is also
characteristic of the process that it is chock-a-block
with things which are incommensurable with one
another, yet which coexist. Some times in discord, at
other times flowing into one another. Time and again
the poem presents, not a single reality which would
enforce a single-keyed response, but that reality and
its converse – or (more subtly) two or three further
realities which chime off the first, in a discordant but
richly complex music of being. That's how the world
is. Nothing comes single; everything skids into the
larger process, and by the very act of existing impli-
cates its incommensurable brothers and lovers and
foes and a joke and grandparents and death and the
dinosaurs, not to mention intergalactic space and a
hangover and spring and the first evolving rampant
protozoa.

And the world provokes incompatible responses
as a matter of daily course. Celebration and elegy
simultaneously; or a fusion of raucous laughter, grief
and awe of an almost unbearable delicacy. Much of
the energy of Purdy's work goes into delivering this
Heraclitean flux intact. Our categorizing minds might
prefer to keep segments of the world in airtight
compartments. But the segments don't cooperate.

There are also poems in which the sense of simulta-

neity goes beyond the normal processes of time alto-
gether. These are poems of ecstasy; they intuit an
eternal now, in which every moment of past, present,
and future participates, in some unfathomable way
surviving its own disappearance.

Often Purdy moves into this ecstatic dimension as
he contemplates the physical world, and finds himself
held in a mysterious under-silence:

> in a pile of old snow
> under a high wall
> a patch of brilliant
> yellow dog piss
> glows, and joins
> things in the mind.
> Sometimes I stand still,
> like a core at the centre
> of my senses, hidden and still –
> All the heavy people,
> clouds and tangible buildings,
> enter and pass thru me:
> stand like a spell
> of the wild gold sunlight,
> knowing the ache stones have,
> how mountains suffer,
> and a wet blackbird feels
> flying past in the rain.
> This is the still centre,
> an involvement in silences –

("Winter Walking")

What is the meaning of this "rare arrival / of something entirely beyond us" ("Time Past / Time Now")?
Sometimes Purdy parses it explicitly as the moment
in which things reveal their perpetual nature:

This incident:
                    sitting with friends
in the chalet restaurant on top of Mount Royal
talking of a tree swaying back and forth in the wind,
leaving no silvery whip marks of its travelling self
                    or proof of passage.
                                        But we say
"That tree will always be there,
flogging the air forever."
                    ("Method for Calling Up Ghosts")

The intuition cannot be translated into conventional thought, of course. And Purdy is so suspicious of mystification of any kind that he mostly backs away from pronouncements on the subject, sometimes from doing anything more than pointing to it cryptically. Often he contents himself with evoking the feel of the eternal moment through the hush and susurration of the words themselves:

They are so different these small ones
their green hair shines
they lift their bodies high in light
they droop in rain and move in unison
toward some lost remembered place
we come from like a question
like a question and the answer
nobody remembers now
no one can remember . . .

                    ("The Nurselog")

Mind you, to concentrate exclusively on these glimpses of an eternal now is to create a one-sided version of the poetry. Purdy is just as concerned with the horror and the boredom of the world as with its murmurs of glory. But those murmurs are worth identifying; they will help us to fathom what makes the process cohere.

3. Polyphony

We move now to one of the most dazzling aspects of Purdy's writing. His command of polyphony, his ability to orchestrate many different voices. No reader can get through twenty lines without becoming aware of the constant shifts of diction and pacing and tone, the squawks and blips as Purdy's consciousness intrudes and recedes, the startling turnarounds from redneck coarseness to a supple middle style to soaring passages of joy and lamentation. Purdy is one of the living masters of voice.

And at this point, we can discern why "finding his voice" was so difficult, and so crucial. The voice of his poems would have to mime the nature of his subject matter – the process, and himself in it. But the nature of the process is to be protean, chameleonic, constantly swerving and bucking and passing into its own opposite in the blink of an eye. Only when the voice of his poetry became as manifold and self-renewing as the process itself would Purdy be able to write the poems that beckoned him. He needed a polyvocal medium, one that could embody his sense of what the world is like.

It would be easy to present five quotations, or fifty, that speak in different voices. And that would indicate Purdy's astonishing tonal range. But it would not demonstrate the most important aspect of the matter – which is not simply that he uses different voices, often in the same poem, but that he's capable of shifting from one to the next in a seamless way, one that mimes a cosmos in which all things flow.

This is not the hard-edge mosaic technique of a Pound, say, where fragment A comes in one voice, fragment B in another, and the two are banged down side by side on the page with no transition. The technique of juxtaposing voices in a discontinuous mosaic issues properly from Pound's vision of things. It has been the main polyphonic tradition in this century; it has even been followed by poets who don't share Pound's vision, but who lack the stature to find their own way of writing polyphonically.

Purdy's technique, which lets him modulate seamlessly through a great range of voices, issues from his vision of the process. The resources of a poetry like this have not been extensively explored. Yet they are crucial to hearing his work on its own wavelength, and hence to understanding it at all. To see how his polyphony works, we should examine the vocal trajectory of one poem from start to finish. To keep things manageable, we'll take a short piece.

LOVE AT ROBLIN LAKE

My ambition as I remember and
I always remember was always
to make love vulgarly and immensely
as the vulgar elephant doth
    & immense reptiles did

in the open air openly
sweating and grunting together
and going
      "BOING   BOING   BOING"
                                          making
every lunge a hole in the great dark
for summer cottagers to fall into at a later date
and hear inside faintly (like in a football
stadium when the home team loses)
ourselves still softly
        going
        "boing   boing   boing"
   as the vulgar elephant doth
       & immense reptiles did
in the star-filled places of earth
that I remember we left behind long ago
and forgotten everything after
on our journey into the dark.

Consider the poem's broad movement in space-time. Purdy starts by conflating his own lovemaking with that of elephants and "immense reptiles," the latter presumably being the dinosaurs. There is already a fusion of times, though merely because the contemporary lover is wishing himself back to a more primitive past. But starting about line eleven, and then much more rapidly in the last four lines, there's an effect like an infinite camera pullback in a movie. Suddenly we see all the traffic of earth – the ambitious lover, the elephants, the long-ago dinosaurs, the planet itself – diminishing to the size of specks, as we unexpectedly pull away from them. This backwards zoom is taking place in time; we are receding into the evolutionary future, away from the "star-filled places of earth" (apparently a time-layer when humans still coupled with the unself-conscious instinct of beasts). And the pullback is also taking place in space; we are receding from the little planet earth into the intergalactic dark, where human and prehuman concerns are so far away they seem both infinitely small and infinitely poignant. The sense of bittersweet awe at the end is unnerving, especially since we have swerved such a great distance in so few lines.

What gives me goose bumps in this poem has to do, I believe, with the way the process of tonal change enacts the process being described. This is the larger truth about Purdy's poetry that we're after. He does not simply write about the process; he keeps miming it in the movement of the poem's voice, its vocal trajectory. Let's retrace "Love at Roblin Lake" with that in mind. For it is clear that the poem starts in one voice, and ends in another. But Purdy's skill at modulating voices is so great that it's far less clear how we got from one to the other.

The piece begins with the speaker as a bit of a bumbler, who gets himself tangled in words at the very outset: "My ambition as I remember and / I always remember was always . . ." After this abrupt little nosedive, the grosseries the speaker is about to deliver about making love "vulgarly and immensely" may give us a yuck or two, may even speak for the sweatily horny strain in us. But given the clumsy, almost coarse tone of his speaking voice, they seem unlikely to rise much above that level. (Few readers will be thinking any of this consciously as they proceed, of course. If

the voice works, it will simply exert a tactful preconscious pressure on our reading, setting the terms in
which we experience the poem as a whole.)

The first surprise comes with the archaic "doth,"
which pops out at the mention of pachyderms and
bygone dinosaurs. With that little tonal blip as the
giveaway, the speaker now appears as a more sophis-
ticated man: as one who enjoys playing roles, including that of a clodhopper – rather than simply being a
clodhopper.

The description of rutting, complete with comic-
book "BOING BOING BOING," picks up the note
of har-de-har comedy again – only to dissolve into the
weird, serpentine, but surprisingly persuasive image
of the phallic trench as a hole in the dark which traps
summer cottagers who turn out to be ourselves as well
now inside a football stadium and raising only muted
cheers because the home team is losing. Wherever the
poem is going, it's clearly nowhere we could have
predicted at the start (a mere dozen lines ago). But
the changing tone of the piece is itself guiding us
through this free, uncharted trajectory in poetic
space. By now the voice has become plain, yet sinewy
and evocative; we have shifted away from the broad,
slapdash tonality of the opening, and though it's not
at all clear where we're headed, the voice now feels
like a trustworthy guide.

Next we discover that we are both inside the
stadium, making love and going "boing," and outside
it, somewhere in undifferentiated space. And our
increasing distance from the stadium action, our ac-

celerating pullback, is mimed as the original "BOING BOING BOING" fades to "boing boing boing." Now the vulgar elephant and the immense reptiles bear a kind of pathos of distance about them, as they echo their earlier appearance. And with the stammer of broken phrases which concludes the poem, we move into an eerie, hedgerow sublime. It may take a few readings before we can analyze where we are, physically or psychically – but at an emotional and imaginative level the heart-wrenched, awestruck tone of the end has already told us:

> going
>   "boing   boing   boing"
> as the vulgar elephant doth
>   & immense reptiles did
> in the star-filled places of earth
> that I remember we left behind long ago
> and forgotten everything after
> on our journey into the dark.

We are watching the funny, sexy, absurd, and poignant dance of mating, performed by one couple, by human beings, by all species that have dwelt on earth. We view them both from within the experience and from a remove that is some place like death, or eternity – where laughter, choked-back tears, and a cosmic hush commingle.

The changing trajectory of voice, together with the sweep of shifting perspectives, has helped Purdy to limn a process in which near and far, past and present, comic and tragic are somehow simultaneous.

4. Tremendum

We have a poetry characterized by zoom perspectives on space-time; by the simultaneity of things that don't jibe; by moments of luminous stillness; and by constant vocal shifts, which guide us through the process according to Purdy. What do they signify?

Purdy gives us a day-to-day world that is unmistakably the cranky, suffering, shades-of-grey place we inhabit. But at the same time he gives us an experience that keeps breaking through in moments of epiphany. This is an encounter with what theologians call mysterium tremendum – holy otherness. An appropriate response to the tremendum is awe, joy, terror, gratitude. We've seen a number of these ecstatic moments, where time seems to lock for the speaker, and the physical world is both utterly present and wholly transparent, a window into some ineffable dimension where he is at once lost and at home. There are many, many more.

For Purdy, such experience of tremendum is always mediated through things of the world. "My Grandfather's Country" ponders the way it impinges through place, and occurs with its own particularity in each locale. In the desert, for example, where " a man can walk and walk into identical distance / like an arrow lost in its own target." Or in the high Arctic, where:

> . . . there are seas in the north so blue
> that a polar bear can climb his own wish and walk the
>   sky

> and wave on wave of that high blue washes over the
>   mind
> and sings to each component part of the hearing blood
> a radiance that burns down the dark buildings of night
> and sings for 24 hours a day of long sea-days . . .

Frequently, as he says in "The Darkness," such experience conveys "some lost kind of coherence / I've never found in people / or in myself for that matter." Thus in "The Beavers of Renfrew," he senses that the beavers still know,

> the secret of staying completely still,
> allowing ourselves to catch up
> with the shadow just ahead of us
> we have lost,
> when the young world was a cloudy room
> drifting thru morning stillness . . .

And sensing this holy otherness in the daily world, he enters the eternal now. Everything that has ever meant itself, ever been at all, seems still to live undiminished in that dimension. Hence everything is simultaneous with everything else – "as if all we are / co-exists in so many forms / we encounter the entire race / of men just by being / alive here" ("Archaeology of Snow").

This eternal now is not situated by Purdy anywhere specifiable: not in a heaven, nor an afterlife, nor art (though it can mediate the intuition), nor his own mind (though it loves to embroider the moment). He has no theories about it; all he can do is recreate its onset on the page, magnificently, as direct experience. Most of the time he scarcely seems to know what to make of its incursions. And the religions which offer a framework for the experience just make him snort atheistically. It's a pure, intuited condition which keeps barging into the flux of the quotidian, without altering the mundane terms in which he lives the rest of his life.

Purdy recreates the daily world as it appears in and out of the light of tremendum. His life work, in all its variety, stands as a series of responses to that central intuition.

And this makes sense of the distinctive elements of process we have observed in his work. It explains the constant zoom perspectives: to whirl from Roblin Lake to the early life of stone 200 million years ago – that is simply to mime the eternal now, in which all time and space are a dance of simultaneity. What's more, in that transcendent moment the heterogeneous things of the world coexist in a kind of charged coherence – without being forced into an abstract unity. So that is how he records them. And to let the poem's voice ripple through a spectrum of changes – that too is to mime the luminous flow in the tremendum, which daily things bespeak in their moments of glory.

That is, the jumps and segues in his poems, their insistence on overlaid or clashing realities, their polyphony – these take their deepest origin from the intuition of mysterium tremendum in the day-to-day world. Purdy's unique way of moving in a poem, and of orchestrating its elements, derives from his fundamental vision of what the world is like. Which is to say, his artistry is mature.

Providing the term is kept free of associations with dogma and churchy attitudes, this vision is properly called religious. But Purdy still doesn't pretend to know what it means that such incandescence lurks in the quotidian. The experience is indelible; its significance is opaque. Questions about God or immortality receive no answer from within the process. The tentative prayer in "The Darkness" is about as close as he's let himself come to addressing the "spirit of everyplace / guardian beyond the edge of chaos" as though it could hear him. And it would be the cheapest effrontery on a reader's part to march in and explain this impulse in his poetry. Or baptize it. Or even label it possessively. My terms for it, "tremendum" and "the eternal now," are meant to honour the mystery, not straitjacket it. And the ecstatic power and incandescent grace which the poetry takes on as it enters the kinetic stillness furnish all the validation that I, for one, could ask.

But Purdy frets at times that he may be simply projecting the movements of his own mind onto the world. "I mistrust the mind-quality that tempts me / to embroider and exaggerate things" ("The Horseman of Agawa"). And it's true; sometimes he himself is clearly inventing the wild leaps which a poem enacts. The result can be a willed, rather frantic exercise.

But the tall tales and goofy exaggerations don't

pretend to be anything other than that. And far from calling in question his deeper treatment of the process, they seem like a coltish retracing of what his intuition already knows. For Purdy writes from a profoundly intuitive imagination, which can tap into some ache and transcendence at the heart of things, and kindle in response. The ecstatic passages of "My Grandfather's Country," "The Beavers of Renfrew," "Night Song for a Woman" – these unmistakably touch grace, whatever its name may be. As do dozens of others. Entering these moments in the poetry, we sense a great hush which sustains the disparate things that are, and renders their all-over-the-map simultaneity and their vocal flow coherent. Such moments don't seem willed by the poet; they seem sponsored by being.

But to end on that lofty note would convey a false impression – not of the vision which animates Purdy's poetry, but of the poems themselves. For one thing, they often report on a daily world which shows no trace of tremendum, and which can be unrelievedly brutal at times. Some of these more humdrum pieces are vigorous and engaging; others are just prosy. But that merely shows that Purdy spends much of his time in a middle state, like the rest of us. He doesn't have nonstop entry to the cosmos of process.

Of greater interest is the compulsion he feels to avoid giving even a sublime poem too much polish, too final and finished a surface. There is an offhandedness, even a slapdash quality, which is clearly an intrinsic part of the way he wants a poem to be. That this is a deliberate policy is evident if we examine his revisions. They can go on for years, decades even, and frequently they polish individual passages to a burnished glow. But often the piece as a whole is left with an in-process, written-while-experienced feel to it; sometimes revision takes it further in that direction. This is an imagination which refuses to be housebroken. And if we approach even a classic Purdy poem too reverently, expecting a rarefied masterpiece, it's likely to light a cigar, tell a bad joke, get up and leave halfway through the conversation. The high style comes and goes as it pleases – as at the end of "Spring Song":

> someone breathed or sighed or spoke
> and everything rearranged itself
> from is to was the white moon tracks
> her silver self across the purple night
> replacing time with a celestial
> hour glass halfway between a girl
> and woman I forgot till she comes jiggling
> back from the dark mailbox at last migawd
> hosanna in the lowest mons veneris I
> will never get to change the goddam oil.

Purdy is a plain man visited by towering intuitions, not a beatified mystic. And his loose-jointed, bantery middle style affords a complex artistic leverage. It lets him acknowledge the long dry stretches between epiphanies – by the very act of including that middle voice. It gives him a way of honouring his plebeian origins, as his highfalutin early verse did not. And it provides a kind of ground bass, against which the moments of tremendum can register more tellingly when they come along. If he does connect with one of those incandescent moments, it will enter a poem whose voice can then modulate or erupt – thanks to his immense improvisational talents – into the high style of the epiphany, and thereby reenact the process it records.

This vocal strategy accounts for much of the unique temper and form of Purdy's work. The trick for a reader is to settle onto a wavelength that can accommodate, as they occur, both the consciously rough-hewn textures and the inflections of the incandescent. Purdy has in effect redefined "a poem" to mean a piece of writing that plays in the space between those boundaries – never in the same way twice. Across the body of his work, that changing vocal play is what we're invited to enjoy.

5. Native Speaking

There are other critical approaches that illuminate Purdy's work. I'll take one more here, considering his poetry as a venture in native speaking.

For half a century, Purdy has been lugging a preoccupation with the spirit of place back and forth across his homeland. The result has been a series of poems about locales and events which assemble into an imaginative map of Canada – not an exhaustive one, but far more complete than any other writer's. Without itemizing individual poems, we can say that he has followed the path of firsthand exploration described in "Transient":

> after a while the eyes digest a country and
> the belly perceives a mapmaker's vision
> in dust and dirt on the face and hands here
> . . .
> and the shape of home is under your fingernails
> the borders of yourself grown into certainty.

These poems of Canadian place and history are a grand gift to the rest of us.

Purdy has "placed" us in subtler ways as well. For one thing, the imaginative journeys he has taken elsewhere in space-time coalesce into a larger map: this time, an experiential record of what one man has discovered in the universe (I have in mind his journeys to other times and species, along with the literal globetrotting). It makes no pretence to being a scholarly world history; the mapmaker's vision is still perceived in the belly and under the fingernails. But the vistas of geological time and interstellar space within which Purdy ranges are breathtaking. And because everything he encounters can be charged with tremendum, can reveal itself as part of the luminous process, his record of journeys in the universe stands as a poetic cosmology, an account of meaningful order.

What's notable is that Purdy focuses the cosmos from the vantage point of his own home. Sometimes this is explicit; in "News Report at Ameliasburg" he transmits a cacophony of war reports from global history, then winds down with a report on sunset in his own small village. But with or without the explicit reference point, a Canada-centred relationship of "there" to "here," of "then" to "now" is defined right in the idiom and perspective of the speaker, who is unmistakably a contemporary Canuck by the name of Al Purdy.

And now there is a new thing on earth: a poetic cosmology focused concentrically around Roblin Lake, southeastern Ontario, Canada, North America, planet earth, all space-time. It does not invalidate visions of order centred elsewhere. But here is a body of major poetry – a muscular, roomy, and persuasive vision of coherence – centred in our own here and now. Such a thing did not exist before.

To write as a native speaker is not just a matter of exploring Canadian places and deeds, however, nor even of mapping the world with Canada as the imaginative centre. At a deeper level it is to embody in words our historic modes of dwelling here – not by describing them at arm's length, but by enacting them on the page. And Purdy has articulated our native reflexes and tensions right in the musculature and movement of his poems. That too has opened imaginative room for us to dwell in.

It would take a whole further essay to explore Purdy's work from this perspective. But let me identify at least some of the native reflexes which inform his work. No one of them is uniquely Canadian, but taken together they have much to do with who we've been here.

The first concerns the tremendum. Throughout history, many things have served as the vehicle for encounter with holy otherness: sexual love, battle, religious contemplation, for example. It is central to our history and imagination in this part of the world that we approach the tremendum through knowing the vast, extreme and eerie land we inhabit. The mystique is strong even among confirmed city dwellers. And Purdy's poems of the land embody that reflex to a singular degree.

A second native reflex is that of instinctively locating our fragile human settlements, even the big cities, in a surrounding space of almost inconceivable magnitude, and as tenuous moments in a field of time which loops back at once to Stone Age humans and out through intergalactic light years. For that is the nature of our dwelling here. The land is vast. Much of the ground our feet or tires traverse was formed eons ago. And the time of white settlement is such a thin patina, usually less than two hundred years in depth, that once we penetrate even a hair's breadth beyond it we are swept into vast reaches of human and prehuman time. In Purdy, that sense of our dwelling contributes to the deep, frequently joyous reflex of temporal and spatial hopscotching that we've already observed.

In "The Runners," a speaker declares, "I think the land knows we are here, / I think the land knows we are strangers." That seems to me the paradigm of a third reflex – a deep and positive ambivalence in the Canadian makeup, which resonates across many aspects of our lives. "The land knows we are here." It antedates us, exerts a claim upon us, and somehow makes us welcome if we come to it knowing our place. We are not free simply to master and remake it according to the dictates of our own wills, as has been a dominant American pattern. We are free to belong to it, gingerly. Yet "the land knows we are strangers." We do not have a history of countless generations here, in which we have domesticated nature and can feel safe in its interpenetration with civilization – as did our forebears in Europe. Both declarations are true to who we are. We exist in their continuing tension, in which we are compelled by both the Old World and the American version of the New – yet neither feels like us. It is a destiny of incomplete or multiple answers, of irony, of perpetual lack of full definition. Purdy's poetry, with its grand articulation of being both strange and at home in this place – a sensitive brawler in taverns, a learned rube – embodies that tension in its very fabric.

A fourth reflex has to do with eloquence, delicacy of feeling, amplitude of spirit. It is central to our social and cultural heritage that these things can be expressed, but only if they are cloaked in defensive irony. And once they have been revealed, we hear them echoing in a still vaster silence, and subsiding into it very quickly again. Purdy's poems enact that reflex, time and again, in their emotional trajectory.

In its embodiment of these deep, historic modes
of being here, his poetry articulates who we are –
places us in our home space – to an unprecedented
degree. In speaking of this, of course, we can't ho-
mogenize all Canadians into a single mould. People
with other modes of dwelling ingrained in their mar-
row are no less Canadian for that. But whether or not
we like every reflex the poems embody, they are many
of us. And so we can move through this poetry
without having to turn ourselves into denizens of
somewhere else, merely to follow its natural lines of
movement. At this profound, almost preconscious
level, Purdy is a supremely accomplished native
speaker.

6. *Purdy's Stature*

How are we to assess Al Purdy? It seems to me
incontrovertible that he is among the finest living
poets, and one of the substantial poets in English of
the century. Of the hundreds of poems he has published, some fifteen or twenty place him in the rank
of poets like D. H. Lawrence, Robert Frost, Dylan
Thomas, Robert Creeley. If we have to realign our
notion of what great poetry looks like to accommodate his best work –and it's part of his achievement
that we do – that is scarcely a novel experience when
a writer of stature comes along.

There's something more as well. If we step back
several paces, we can find a broader perspective in

which to situate Purdy, one that sheds fuller light on his achievement.

From the sixteenth century on, the imperial nations of Europe spread their languages and cultural paradigms around the planet: English, French, Spanish, Portuguese, and to a lesser extent Dutch. For better and worse. And during the twentieth century, after a long colonial period, literature in those languages became polycentric, as the former colonies found their voices – rivaling and sometimes surpassing the imperial centres. The most impressive contemporary example is that of Spanish and Portuguese writing in Latin America, but the process has been repeated around the globe, in recent decades with gathering potency.

This has not just been a matter of poets and novelists in the ex-colonies learning to write well in the fashion of their erstwhile mentors. The language of the metropolitan imagination has had to be unlearned, even as it was being learned from. A long hard struggle of independence has been necessary for writers of the hinterlands to imagine their own time and place, to become articulate as native speakers. The titans have been those who first broke through to indigenous articulacy, who subverted and recast the forms of the metropolitan imagination so as to utter the truths of the hinterland. Generally they've done so with a rare fusion of high artistry and folk, even populist imagination. It's clear that Whitman, Melville, Neruda, Garcia Marquez are among the founders who've claimed a nation's patrimony this

way, and in the process recast the imaginative vocabu-
lary of their medium. Without pretending to exhaustive knowledge of the subject, I suspect their number
also includes Dario, Amado, Guillen, Asturias, Ce-
saire, Miron, Senghor, Walcott.

In the case of countries colonized by England, the
situation is complicated one stage further. American
writers made their breakthrough to native speaking
very early, in the nineteenth century. In the result,
American literature went on to such strengths that by
the mid-twentieth century, Anglophone writers elsewhere had to free themselves from the hegemony of
both Britain and the United States. Such a situation
does not exist in French, Spanish, or Portuguese. But
that anomaly recognized, the challenge of speaking
native among English-speaking writers in Africa, India, Canada, Australia, the Caribbean, and elsewhere
has been parallel to that faced by a Neruda or a
Senghor.

And that situates Al Purdy in a wider context. He
has been one of the giants of the recurrent process in
which, language by language and country by country
over the last seventy years, the hinterlands of empire
have broken through to universal resonance by learning to speak local. Purdy has claimed, and in many
ways created, an indigenous imaginative patrimony
for English Canada.

To say that is not to denigrate Canadian poets
whose excellence is of other kinds – Irving Layton and
Margaret Avison, for a start. Emily Dickinson wasn't
called to be Whitman, nor Vallejo, Neruda. But in his

rootedness, his breadth, and his impulse to forge a native idiom for the imagination, Purdy is one of a distinct breed: the heroic founders, who give their people a voice as they go about their own necessities.

Of course, not all giants are equal in stature. And seen in that lofty company, Purdy may be one of the lesser titans. But it is among their number that he must be counted.

It is a matter of fact that readers abroad have scarcely begun to discover Al Purdy. Or more accurately, have not yet taken the crucial first step – of hearing this hinterland idiom on its own wavelength, as an instrument capable of genius, at once familiar and foreign. But such tone-deafness in the metropolis is an old story. It is the hard luck of London and New York, which time will rectify.

Meanwhile, for those who can read Purdy on his own wavelength, his poetry is a windfall and a blessing.

AL PURDY AMONG THE POETS

SAM SOLECKI

Somewhere in the late 1970s, Al Purdy's poems began to make more open use in his own work of the poets and poems he admired. It was almost as if he had become sufficiently confident in his status as a poet to occasionally acknowledge his sources. Contrary to the popular view, nurtured on too many public readings of "At the Quinte Hotel," his poems rarely lack allusions, echoes and quotations. The very early "In Mid-Atlantic," for instance, echoes Hopkins and Thomas, "The Cariboo Horses" owes something to Neruda, Hughes and Larkin, and "The Viper's Muse" uses Eliot's "Journey of the Magi" and Browning's "Home-Thoughts from the Sea." There's nothing unusual in this. As Eliot pointed out nearly a century ago, poets borrow, steal and plagiarize. This is one of the ways that they relate the individual talent to the tradition.

What is unusual is when a poet like Purdy contin-ues to do this while also incorporating lines from poems that he admires, letting them stand side by side with his own. "Touchings," in his penultimate collec-tion, quotes at some length from Yeats, MacLeish, Lawrence, W.J. Turner, Auden and Rilke. It's one of several poems of the past two decades – the most elaborate is "Bestiary [II]: ABC of P" – with what you might call a genealogical thrust; the poet, in the autumn and winter phase of his career, uses poems to write a family tree, to declare filiation. The manuscript of *The Cariboo Horses* shows that Purdy had wanted to do something similar as early as 1965 with the following dedication: "To: Charles Bukowski, A.E. Housman, W.H. Auden, Robinson Jeffers, Catullus and Callimachus of Alexandria." Curiously, the book appeared without a dedication, almost as if Purdy, despite the first flush of success, wasn't ready to show how really bookish a poet he was nor to acknowledge some of his debts. A decade later he would write that "Northrop Frye's dictum that poems are created from poems seems to me partially true, in the sense that if other people's poems hadn't been written you couldn't have written your own. In that sense, what each of us writes balances and juggles the whole history of literature . . ." (A Handful of Earth, 1977).

And it's some of that balancing and juggling that I want to discuss.

Yeats

Though there were poets like Lawrence and Auden from whom he learned more and whose work he borrowed from and echoed more often, in Purdy's private anthology, Yeats's poems were set apart. He knew that there were many other great poets, but to

use the Laurentian phrase he didn't "know it along
the blood." He liked to recite parts of poems like
"Sailing to Byzantium" or "No Second Troy" but he
was slightly in awe of them, as if for him they represented another order of poetic creativity. He borrows
from or echoes Yeats as early as 1948 ("Abstract
Plans") and the papers contain an unfinished "Among
School Children", but he only engages the Irish poet
in what are minor poems, almost as if he can't master
him, subdue him to his own style. Even when he tries
to pay tribute to him in "Bestiary [II]", the result is
one of the weaker stanzas in the poem:

> Yeats for Maud Gonne,
> and those little glittering gay eyes
> of the Chinese man: and because of him,
> a feeling that greatness still lives.

Neither here nor in the later "Yeats" can he translate
his feelings and critical intuitions into poetry. And his
"Among School Children," with its allusion to "Sailing to Byzantium," remained a very rough, unfinished
draft. The poet who called himself "The King of the
Cats" when Swinburne died in 1909 was beyond him
and, as far as he was concerned, beyond almost
everyone else.

Carman (with Noyes and Turner)

It would be only a slight exaggeration to claim that
Purdy spent nearly two decades, from the mid-1930s
to the early 1950s, writing his way out from under

Carman's cape. Even in his collections of the 1990s, an occasional lyric like "Springtime" recalls the Confederation poet who turned him on to poetry in high school. His first half-dozen unpublished collections, all typed and hand-bound in leather, mimic Carman to the point that occasionally you can't be sure that pastiche isn't plagiarism. "Bliss Carman," written in 1942 and collected in a manuscript titled "Song of the Restless Ones," ends:

> And then the Lord of April
> Looked on you at your play
> He watched your fancies forming
> And gave you words to say.
>
> You roamed the sun splashed inlets
> Past islands fresh and free
> And watched those blue battalions
> The never aging sea.

Purdy was twenty-two years old, enlisted in the RCAF and with years to go before he would write a passable poem.

It's conventional wisdom, encouraged by some of Purdy's own comments in his letters and essays, that Carman and the kind of poetry he represents were completely left behind when Purdy remade himself as a writer through the 1940s and 1950s. When he writes about Carman in the 1980s and 1990s, he usually does so with a combination of admiration and embarrassment. In *Reaching for the Beaufort Sea,* for instance, he lists Carman among the poets he loved and memorized in school:

So I memorized and memorized at school, much of it
lost in the mind's overflow. I immersed myself in Carman, Carman, Carman . . . And Browning, although I
can't remember the last lines of "Home Thoughts" any
longer. And Tennyson,

And I dipped into the future
As far as human eye could see
Saw a vision of the world
And all the wonder that would be.

Remember, remember. And leave all the mistakes of
quotation where they belong, uncorrected: and the
lines glow like dead fireflies in your memory.

He also quotes snatches of G.K. Chesterton,
Hilaire Belloc, W.J. Turner and Oliver St. John
Gogarty, none of whom are much read today except
by specialists in the field, though, it is worth recalling,
Karl Shapiro refers to Turner in his Essay on Rhyme,
while Chesterton's "Lepanto" was a set text in Ontario high schools in the early 1960s. Letting himself
go and not worrying about modernist critical ortho-
doxy, Purdy evokes in the above passage lovingly and
sentimentally the lost world of the poetry on which
he was nurtured and which, during a crucial decade
in his development, he had to turn his back on in
order to make himself a poet. Reaching for the
Beaufort Sea, like the essays on Kipling and Carman
(see "Starting from Ameliasburg"), offers an un-
ashamedly subjective rewriting of literary history in
which Carman, Alfred Noyes ("The Highwayman"),
Chesterton, Belloc, Gogarty and the completely for-

gotten W.J.Turner ("Epithalamium for a Modern Wedding") are as important as Byron, Browning and Tennyson, and Chesterton's "The Battle of Lepanto" is as memorable as any poem in the century. Other than Auden, I can't think of another modern poet who writes as affectionately and strongly of poets normally, and justifiably, omitted from the canon and given at best cursory treatment in histories of modern poetry. And not even Auden would have been willing to declaim and defend this stanza from Turner: "I have stared upon a dawn / And trembled like a man in love, / A man in love I was, and I / Could not speak and could not move."

For Purdy, Carman is like a painting once popular, critically respectable (something by William Bouguereau or Puvis de Chavannes) and even loved which one realizes has passed completely out of fashion. His ambivalent loyalty to him is that of a student who has surpassed his master and now clearly sees his limitations without, however, rejecting him for them. For Purdy, Carman is the predecessor who, in the end, represents a road he had to turn his back on, though it must be emphasized that doesn't mean that Carman and the poetry he represents are completely absent from Purdy's later work. Not the least of the ironies in his career is that Purdy could not have found his eclectic mature poetic had he not made the mistake of following Carman for longer than he wants to remember.

I would even suggest that Purdy is one of the few contemporary poets writing predominantly in free verse who is nostalgic for the conservative past, saddened by the fact that his poems – because of free verse – cannot be memorized and recited and therefore cannot be literally as memorable as Carman's. I recall a dinner in Toronto in the early 1990s at which Josef Skvorecky and Purdy took turns reciting, in Czech and English respectively, long stretches of their favourite poems. First Jaroslav Seifert, then Bliss Carman; Jiri Orten followed by W.J. Turner; and so on. On the basis of that spontaneous public performance I have little doubt that Purdy would agree with Derek Walcott's comment that to quote from memory "is the greatest tribute to poetry."

MacLeish

Purdy, like Mark Strand, always wished that he had written Archibald MacLeish's "You, Andrew Marvell." It was one of the poems that he liked to recite, and his admiration for it never wavered. Because of it and "You Also, Gaius Valerius Catullus" he could forgive the hundreds of dull pages in MacLeish's *Collected Poems*.

In the end, unable to be the poem's author, he decided to pay homage to it by incorporating it twice in his own work, first in "Bestiary [II]" (1984) and subsequently in "Touchings" (1994). The former is more ambitious and more memorable.

> You, Gaius Valerius Catullus
> " – here face down beneath the sun":

an absent friend, lost in the centuries' dust
next door, just stepped out for a minute –

By quoting from the poem he was able to include
MacLeish in his catalogue of favourite poets without
devoting a stanza to him, without, that is, overrating
him.

Birney

He probably wrote as many letters to Birney as to any
other Canadian writer. In the early years, from 1947
on, Birney not only read and responded to his poems,
he also helped him continue his education in modern
poetry. In an undated letter from the mid-1960s, for
example, Birney offers an off the cuff lecture on
influence in Canadian poetry; he lists twenty Canadian poets and then indicates whose voice he can hear
in their poetry: A.M. Klein (Eliot), P.K.Page (Ander-
son, Thomas and Barker), Livesay (Auden, Sitwell,
the Symbolistes).

When Purdy lists the poets who have been important to him, he usually includes Birney and Layton.
The introduction to *Being Alive* has the following
catalogue:

> I suppose that the people I've admired as writers also
> inhabit what I've written. The most notable of those
> to me is the D.H. Lawrence of *Birds, Beasts and Flow-
> ers*. But a host of others: Neruda and Vallejo, James
> Dickey and Robinson Jeffers, some French poets
> whose names I always misspell, Catullus, Chesterton

and W.J. Turner (whoever heard of Turner these
days!) And Dylan Thomas especially. Of course also
Birney, Klein, Dudek, Atwood, Lee, Layton, Cohen,
Newlove and Acorn. Almost everybody. In fact, I think
everyone influences me. Thank you.

On the evidence of the poems, however, Birney's
direct influence was minimal. Purdy admired
"David," "El Greco: Espolio" and "Bushed" and even
wrote an unpublished essay on the last, but he borrowed little beyond the following: the archaic spell-
ings in the early "Flies in Amber" may owe something
to "Anglosaxon Street" and "Mappemounde"; "On
Canadian Identity" borrows the phrase "A high
school land" from "Canada, A Case History: 1945";
and a passage in "Lament for the Dorsets" echoes the
lineation and phrasing of "El Greco: Espolio."

More important was the dialogue about poetry
that continued in person and on paper for nearly four
decades. In 1955, for example, he reports on his
struggle with one of the fathers of High Modernism:

> I am knee-deep in Ezra Pound at the moment; but his
> images are literary for the most part. An odd blend of
> simplicity and erudition. But at the present time I sim-
> ply cannot read *The Cantos*. They are not coherent
> enough or continuous. But I revel in the Faber ed. of
> *Selected Poems*, the one with the Eliot preface.

The letters also contain the earliest examples of
Purdy's attempts to work out a poetics. He comments
on the canon, the Anglo-American tradition and contemporary poetry; he speculates about influence, me-

tre, rhythm, rhyme and the relationship between form and content. And like a good teacher, Birney hears him out, asks questions, offers suggestions for further reading, and occasionally corrects, as he does in the following paragraph commenting on a draft of a poem that mentions Oedipus.

> . . . you miss my point. The poem glances at an incestuous rape of daughter by father, and you refer to him as a possible 'shamed Oedipus' if he is exposed. Oedipus never had anything to do with his daughter, only with his mother, sexually. You reference is a gaffe.

The dialogue lasted until Birney's collapse in the 1980s.

Layton

Layton occasionally drifts into the Birney-Purdy correspondence. In 1959, for instance, Al, living in Montreal, informs Birney in Vancouver about Layton's most recent success:

> Layton is here selling in the stores like Billy Graham or Norman Vincent Peale. 5,000 copies of this ed. of *Red Carpet* . . . Ever meet him? Wonderful experience to see the naked ego like an unruptured maidenhead floating in the living room void . . . and he knows, he just knows, that he is the great one, the poet who will top Milton and Blake and Yeats and who do you like? He said so . . . and there you are. But in a sense I love the guy, so improbable, grotesque, and despite his ability somehow wrong. Why? It's all too bloody trite and rehearsed . . . so much assurance and so little doubt. . . . but I assign him a large statue in my private

Tussaud's, and think to myself I should not bloody
well have this uncertainty. I should know he's good (as
I know he is) and great . . . well . . .

If he was comfortable almost from the start with
Birney, one has the impression that he was slightly in
awe of Layton. The difference may have been the
result of his sense that Layton was the stronger and
more original poet. He always admired Birney's
work, but as soon as he found his voice he began to
measure himself against Layton. His review of the
Layton's *Collected Poems* in 1967 is the equivalent of
a declaration of independence, though a shift in the
relationship is hinted at in the unpublished 1964
parody "Irving Layton's Immortal Ode to Joyous Life
and Enhancing Hebraic Love in the Wisconsin Glacial
Periods of Rosedale."

In the preface to his 1986 *Collected Poems,* Purdy
mentions only Layton and D.H.Lawrence as signifi-
cant influences – "examples not tutors." In calling
Lawrence and Layton "examples, not tutors" I suspect that Purdy wants to emphasize that in confront-
ing them he managed to avoid imitating them and,
thus, to find his own voice through his reading of their
poetry. He is able simultaneously to indicate indebt-
edness as well as freedom, the tradition and the
individual talent. The importance of his encounter
with both cannot be underestimated, and each, in
different ways, has influenced his major work though,
paradoxically, without leaving his voice on it. Each,
however, left a residue of images and echoes.

The force of Layton's presence can be gauged from Purdy's descriptions of him both in his poetry and in his prose. His earliest attempt to turn Layton into poetry is "The Great Man," an unpublished poem from 1958. He sent it to Birney and admitted that "The Great Man is, of course, Layton." A playful, affectionate and perceptive poem, it presents the title character from four viewpoints: his wife's, a friend's, a critic's and his own. The wife recognizes that everything in the poet's life, including herself and the children, is secondary to words and poetry; the critic describes his as "almost a Canadian Catullus / With Freudian guilt"; and the poet thinks of himself as "that Prince from Serendip / Who was what his mind held." In "Disconnections," Purdy looks back across three decades after their first meeting:

> . . . Layton was kingpin for me. Visits to the Côte St-Luc cottage were occasions of subdued excitement. With a face like that of some Semitic Buddha, he would listen with close attention when you tried to explain an opinion or had a point to make . . . he pontificated about world literature and his own genius, a gift to grateful mankind – it was like listening to God . . . Layton was extremely erudite. He devoured critical books that I found boring. Nietzsche was an exemplar; a candle for D.H. Lawrence burned sometimes in a living-room niche at Côte St-Luc. I saw Layton once, hurrying along a sunlit afternoon sidewalk, face buried in a book, oblivious to everything else. I didn't speak to him; that would have amounted to wrecking a ten-mile train of thought. I loved the man.

The hyperbole seems to beg for deflation, but it's

worth noting that Purdy doesn't provide it: his admiration and affection for Layton shine through the intervening decades. Though the essay also registers, with some reluctance, Purdy's reservations about Layton's later poetry, it leaves little doubt that Layton was important to him in three ways. He continued Purdy's education in modern poetry; by his own example he showed Purdy that modern poetry of a high standard was being written in Canada; and he taught him that a Canadian poet could be Laurentian without simply imitating Lawrence's world view or his poetic.

In any relationship between poets, there are also various intangibles. Simply to be taken seriously by Layton in 1956 must have been of enormous importance to an unknown poet like Purdy, a thirty-six year old who had failed at almost everything he had attempted. The effect of a letter from a major poet as encouraging as this one (July 1, 1956), responding to some recent poems, is probably incalculable:

> I thought them the very best things you've done up to now, though you may not agree with me. I think you've at last found the form suitable to your free-swinging imagination. Not only that, it permits you to comment as well as to imagine. What you need is a form that allows you lots of elbow room, to slide in and out of your many moods and complexities, your passionate uncertainties.

What's remarkable here is Layton's anticipation of some of the comments that Purdy's later readers will make in response to later poems answering more closely to Layton's description. It's as if Layton writes in response to poems he thinks Purdy is capable of writing rather than to those that will be collected a year later in *Emu, Remember!* Whatever the case, it's a remarkably generous and prescient critical perform-ance in which Layton seems to foresee Purdy's Laurentian turn. It's also worth noting what is missing in Layton's letters and in Purdy's memories of their encounters: the older poet never tried to refashion Purdy into a poet in his own image. Some of Layton's images and metaphors will have a second life in Purdy's poems, more on this below, but not his voice and poetics.

According to *Reaching for the Beaufort Sea* – written over thirty years after the crucial encounter – Layton was also important simply because he created the impression through his work and personality "that anything was possible" and that "we were all great writers, or would be."

In the 1960s and 1970s, after Purdy had won the Governor General's Award for *The Cariboo Horses* (1965), I suspect that Layton may have been equally important as the one obviously "strong" poet against whom Purdy measured himself. Layton could be imi-tated and reacted against. And in contrast to some of the other "contenders" – Avison, Dudek, Souster – he was so obviously "there" as a challenging presence that could not be avoided. There is evidence of Purdy's early wrestle with Layton in several poems from the 1950s, most obviously "Poem" (*Emu, Re-member!*) and "At Roblin Lake" (*The Crafte so Long to Lerne*). The first ends with two images borrowed from Layton's "The Birth of Tragedy." Images from Layton's early poems also reappear in the late seventies in "Starlings" and "On Realizing He Has Written Some Bad Poems." In the first, Purdy reaches back to "The Cold Green Element" for Layton's image of "the labels of medicine bottles"; and in the second he returns to Layton's "brilliant / hunchback" and changes him into "the jewelled hunchback in my head."

Looking back on their generation, I have a hunch that Purdy can only be understood in Canadian poetry facing Layton whose poems of the 1950s showed him a way of becoming a modern poet without giving up either the poetry he had grown up with or the poetry of his self-education.

Guthrie

One of the first times that we talked at some length about poetry after I started dropping in at Ameliasburg, he brought out a copy of Ramon Guthrie's *Maximum Security Ward: 1964-1970* and asked me if I'd read it. I told him that not only had I not read it, I had never heard of Guthrie. A variant of this scene happened a few times over the next few years, and on each occasion I could tell by the self-satisfied smile that he enjoyed being able to teach the prof something new. Chalk up one for the auto-didacts.

A few years later, around 1993 when I was writing

my book about him, I told him during a phone call that I thought he had borrowed a couple of images in "In the Caves," his poem about a cave artist, from Guthrie's "The Making of the Bear" and "This Stealth." He chuckled and said, "I was wondering whether you'd spot that."

Lawrence

Lawrence, the other "example" not "tutor," is as Purdy has repeatedly acknowledged in poems, essays and letters, the single most important literary figure in his work and life: "my ultimate mentor."

> [Lawrence's] *Birds, Beasts and Flowers* actually changed the way I thought inside a poem. One is not conscious of thinking while doing it, at least I am not . . . Lawrence knew that a poem could say anything . . . So that he wrote his life in his poems, and toward the end of his life he wrote his death. When a poet – myself in this case – is influenced enough by Lawrence, then he escapes all influence, including Lawrence. After DHL, all other influences merge seamlessly into your own work.

Lawrence's role in Purdy's development is fascinating precisely because until the late 1970s and 1980s it is so inconspicuous in the major poems in which he found the voice that would deepen and expand in range over the remainder of his career.

Since Lawrence is obviously more important to Purdy than to Layton as a poet – Layton tends to value him as a prophet or sage – I have the impression that

Purdy could only let himself write out of and about
Lawrence when he was sufficiently established as a
poet, sufficiently confident in the stature of his own
work and in the poetic and view of life he had
developed in response to Lawrence's example. A
decade after the three great books of the 1960s – *The
Cariboo Horses, North of Summer* and *Wild Grape
Wine* – he seems to have felt that he could engage his
mentor openly on common ground without the
"anxiety of influence." These are poems of dialogue
with the poet who had shown him how to write a
"poetry of the present" with a line and prosody
adequate to the vitality, variability, tone, timbre and
amplitude of his own voice – what Layton had called
his "free-swinging imagination" and "passionate un-
certainties." These poems could only have been written when he had the confidence that they could stand
side by side with Lawrence's without being over-
whelmed by them. In other words the Laurentian
poems are simultaneously homage and assertion of
independence. This seems to me particularly true in
"Lawrence's Pictures" and "The Death of DHL"
where Lawrence's words and images are taken and
placed within a monologue whose voice is Purdy's.
Here Purdy's wrestle with the great dead (Harold
Bloom's phrase) results in the momentary establishing
of an equivalence between the two poets as their
voices meet in an implicit dialogue. The risk, of
course, is that the language of the canonical poet will
overwhelm the successor as often happens even when
a minor poet simply quotes a major one. How many

contemporary poems have been exposed as second-rate simply by ill-advised epigraphs or quotations from Rilke, Yeats or Stevens?

Acorn

Among the things in life that he had difficulty accepting were Milton Acorn's suffering in his later years and death. Acorn had been there in the 1950s to help him with the building of the house in Ameliasburg and with his difficult apprenticeship to poetry. In the preface to the 1986 *Collected,* he mentions him side by side with Lawrence and Layton: "Milton Acorn gets in there somewhere as well; I learned from him both how to write and how not to write. (Very few people can teach you opposite things at the same time.)" I always had the feeling that when he spoke about Acorn, he was in some complex sense also talking about himself. Their differences were obvious, but they had enough in common – self-education; poverty and failure; shyness and dark moods; the mutual struggle with "the crafte so long to lerne" – that looking at Acorn he must have sometimes felt he was looking into a mirror.

In conversations about Canadian poets, he would almost always bring up Acorn's name and quote a stanza or two from "I've Tasted My Blood" or "Sky's Poem for Christmas." He wrote two poems about him, "House Guest" (two versions) and "In the Desert," and each is an elegy. I once told Al that I thought

"The Dead Poet," which is addressed to the brother stillborn two years before his birth, was also in some oblique and mysterious way about Acorn. He chuckled and said that had never occurred to him, but he could see why someone might think it.

Rilke

Rilke fascinated him from at least the early 1960s. "Muskoke Elegiac," a sequence of unpublished poems from around 1965, has a couplet that catches something of his ambivalent attitude: "O Rilke, work your lovely fraud / for we who are your music must applaud." He read him first in the Leishman / Spender translations which he remembered clearly enough that he would argue with me in the early 1990s about the forced closing rhyme in "Autumn Day":

> He'll not build now, who has no house awaiting.
> Who's now alone, for long will so remain:
> sit late, read, write long letters, and again
> return to restlessly perambulating
> the avenues of parks when leaves downrain.

(In 1994, in "Touchings", he would quote the second and third lines but in Stephen Mitchell's translation.) When I asked him in 1992 why he was fascinated with Rilke and kept coming back to him, he wrote back that "[Rilke] slips thru my fingers too. Dunno what made him tick. He was, of course, the complete 'artist' and I'm not sure what that consists of apart from human being. He kept writing and writing tho and that I envy. (I haven't written a poem since October, and that's a long time for me!) I read a bit of his novel *(The Notebooks of Malte Laurids Brigge)*, which seemed almost incomprehensible."

Throughout the nineties, he would continue to worry Rilke. *To Paris Never Again*, his last collection, contained "House Party," a version of the Alcestis story that acknowledged its source in Rilke's poem. And "In the Rain," one of many death-haunted late poems, mentions Rilke in the closing stanza.

> I will sleep my way into death
> searching for an instant in dreams
> to find that moment again
> for that face reconstituted and intact again
> with all past ages echoing
> from microscopic amoeba to Rilke

Ironically, a poem about coming to terms with the inevitability of death culminates in Rilke, against whose accepting attitude to death Purdy had raged in a 1971 letter to Birney: "Rilke is sort of 'accept,' 'accept!' which I don't like. (I'm fucked if I'll accept a lot of things.) A kind of roseate look at depression and death. One accepts, but dammit one doesn't have to like it, stoicism is too damn Greek for me. I want to be the cat yowling on the backyard fence sometimes. In fact, I ought to write some of this in a poem."

Sam Solecki's most recent book is *The Last Canadian Poet: An Essay on Al Purdy*. Some paragraphs in this article first appeared there.

WHAT A LIFE

LINDA ROGERS

When Al was in a teasing mood, which was often, he would quote some not so great lines of poetry written by my grandmother's cousin, Bliss Carman, "Make me over Mother April, when the sap begins to stir . . . " In the end, April got him. The not always good boy of Canadian poetry died on Good Friday, when miracles happen and men who smoked cigars and drank beer get into heaven. Earlier in the week while riding to Moloka'i in a small plane, which parted the clouds in front of it, moving to the light, I remembered a near death experience and said to myself "You're in, Al!"

In fact, the trip was beautiful. Al died in his sleep, lines of poetry, no doubt, floating in his populous brain.

When we got back, my husband and I went to the cemetery with Eurithe to look at headstones. Rick sketched a bench, where readers could rest against lines from his last poem:

> This is where I came to
> when my body left its body
> and my spirit stayed
> in its spirit home.

In the end, the bench became a book with the quote

on the cover and *Voice of the Land*, an award we presented at home just a few days before he died, written on the spine because the cemetery was going to charge its most eloquent inhabitant for a double-wide and Al was always careful with his money and his praise.

There are many Al Purdy stories, but my favourite, most personal one is about both our shortcomings. I am a little deaf. Al, who always cherished his wife, Eurithe, but came close to never admitting it until the angel of death made it clear he had better, was fretting about her, driving to Victoria from their summer home in Ameliasburg, Ontario. "I hope she doesn't run into snow and ice," said the guilty poet who had enjoyed a comfy flight west courtesy of the Canada Council, jingling the coins in his pocket. "Oh Al," I replied, "even if she does run into someone nice, she won't be interested. She's not used to it."

On Al's eightieth birthday, in 1998, Susan Musgrave refused to host his party as she had in the past, because he had been too crabby and hurt her feelings. Someone else took over the job and Susan brought the cake, making that concession to an old familial friendship. This time, he was good, didn't put his large shoe in one of Susan's well-crafted cakes, a facsimile typewriter for the stubborn writer who never conceded to cybertime. A bunch of the "girls," Musgrave, Marilyn Bowering, Patricia Young and myself, draped ourselves around the old lion for a birthday photo and Al lay down like a lamb. Do lambs purr?

For our gift, my husband and I brought a copy of Ted Hughes' *Birthday Letters* and some freefall poems my students had written around a list of words I pulled out of Al's life and poetic canon; among them "beer," "mattress," "hotel," "boxcar," "breast" and "brat." The kids were thrilled to write this close to genius. Al loved the poems, reverent, irreverent reactions to his "larger than" life in the Canadian literary landscape.

It wasn't long after that party we heard a lifetime of smoking was having its terrible vengeance. Al was a big man and the lungs filling up with cancer must have been larger than average because it is the amazing sostenuto of his voice that has made him one of the most extraordinary narrative poets of this century, in and out of the country of his birth.

Alfred Wellington Purdy, a late Christmas gift born to middle-aged parents December 30, 1918, was the cherished, he admits "spoiled," only child of a woman who had known loss.

> I was altered in the placenta
> by the dead brother before me
> who built a place in the womb
> knowing I was coming;
> he wrote words on the walls of flesh
> painting a woman inside a woman
> whispering a faint lullaby
> that sings in my blind heart still.
>
> ("The Dead Poet")

Altered by the former occupant of the most luxurious room in a house dedicated to God, he was announced by a fanfare heard all over the county. On Thanksgiving Day, 1918, the British Chemical Company's munitions factory north of Trenton exploded, interrupting Al's peaceful sojourn in the "timeless calm and measureless peace" of his mother's womb, and auguring an explosive life.

Coddled and dressed as Little Lord Fauntleroy for photographs, Al was the distanced special child of elderly parents and one eccentric grandparent. His mother, stern and religious, poured all her love into this awkward vessel. The other mythological figure of his childhood was the large grandfather who took him by the hand, walked him down the street and introduced him to the "life of men" that characterized his own journey through the larger landscape of Canada and the world.

His uncomfortable life in pants smaller than he was was expanded by the vicarious world of books and infantile writing. In his autobiography, he describes running into "the sort of heroic drivel I was writing myself with Robin Hood and the Norse myths. Many years later, reading Stan Dragland's *Wilson MacDonald's Western Tour,* I chuckled over the bit where MacDonald locks the doors in his reading hall so that the audience couldn't escape when he sold his books." No doubt.

These days, Al would have been called a "nerd" had he been more apparently academic. In truth, he was a "geek," gangly and as awkward with other children as he was at sports and the academic curriculum. Clown/actor Stuart Nemtin's mother, who went to school with Purdy, described him as "a loner, who was followed to school by stray cats." Al, never overly agreeable, insists it had to be his dog, Gyp, but the cat image sticks. Perhaps those unhappy school days are the reason the autodidact was so passionately anti-intellectual. If you wanted to raise his blood pressure, you just had to ask Al, who knew just about everything, a pompous brain question.

In spite of his aversion to directed learning, he accumulated a splendid library and read every book in it. One of Purdy's favourite pastimes was the inexpensive acquisition of rare books. While Al hunted first editions, his independent wife, Euriche, stalked the fine china of which she is passionately fond. The miracle of Al's life was his parallel relationship with a woman of spirit, who let him be himself but somehow maintained her own integrity.

In *Reaching for the Beaufort Sea*, the autobiography with its title taken from the song by Stan Rogers, a favourite composer of Purdy, who favoured men's voices in poetry and music, he described the hilarious mating procedure, during which he "interviewed" several young ladies with predictable results until he finally lay down and "smooched" with Euriche in a hideout contaminated by dog droppings.

This ambivalence about romance presented in the most unromantic context set the tone for six decades of marriage in which the most durable Euriche endured what can only be described as a rocky ride through the dangerous terrain of poetry, a journey punctuated by arguments and separations and held together by a fierce devotion to the higher purpose, which is poetry.

> I walk faster than my wife,
> then have to stop and wait for her:
> "It isn't much farther,"
> I say encouragingly
> and note that our married life
> is about to end in violence,
> judging from her expressionless expression.
>   ("Over the Hills in the Rain, My Dear")

That "expressionless expression," which I call "inscrutable," is the blank page upon which much great poetry has been written. Eurithe, who may have lied about her age when she met the tall airman at the beginning of World War Two and married him shortly after, is the matrix in which the raw rhyming poetry of the early years became the mature voice. His dialogue with her, "I act," he said putting his hand around her wrist, "she reacts," is the script for narrative poetry that tells the story of human life, birth, copulation and death.

The fearful boy who was close to his overpowering mother found in his wife a woman who is strong, more than a match for his sometimes misanthropic behaviour, loyal and having the humour necessary for spending a lifetime with an only child devoted to his muse. Luckily, Eurithe was powerful enough to capture the muse in her own sexual presence and to control the poetic explosions with irony.

One of many children, Eurithe became the mother of poetry and one son, who had to struggle for his rightful place in a family dominated by words. When Al gave up the day jobs, running a cab company and working for minimum wage in a mattress factory, Eurithe, who had once dreamed of studying medicine, worked to support the family and also helped in the physical labour of building their own home on Roblin Lake at Ameliasburg, where:

> The pike and bass are admirably silent
> about such things, and keep their
> erotic moments a mensa e toro
> in cold water. After which, I suppose,
> comes the non-judicial separation

("At Roblin Lake")

There were separations, affairs, trips abroad and reprises of the depression journey in boxcars to the West Coast of Canada, a geographical theme that parallels the marriage. He was east, she was west and they were irresistibly drawn to one another and sometimes repelled. This is the tension in the poetry, an organic process described in *Reaching for the Beaufort Sea*, "Writing them was – and I guess still is –a condition of living for me. Not like breathing or my heart beating, which sounds literarily pretentious anyway. I take writing for granted. The words "I must write a poem" never come into my head. I just do it." The pull to poetry was as basic as the attraction to women.

One sunny afternoon, testing me, thirty years younger and between marriages, and the security of his own durable relationship, the fundamentally conservative son of a pillar of the United Church swooped in the driveway as I got into my car. "What would you do if I kissed you?" he asked. I gave him my own version of the expressionless expression. "Oh nothing, just tell Eurithe," I said, and that was that, both of us satisfied with my answer.

Friendship with Al Purdy was like going for a ride in a cantankerous car. It was always an adventure. We stalked the wild asparagus along ditches in Southern Ontario, (I won't say throwing beer bottles out of the only window that rolls down, but that was the feeling), shared the intimate secrets of many pompously famous individuals, (this at my peril, because Al loved to repeat all MY stories, even the ones he promised not to), and standing beside him at some of his own pompously famous moments, letting the air out of them later.

On the occasion of his investiture to the Order of Ontario, an honour he shared with ballerina Celia Franca, wrestler Gene Kinisky, and sprinter Ben Johnson, before the scandals (I felt his muscles and marvelled), Al was forced into a dinner jacket and a pair of ill-fitting shoes he and Eurithe had picked up at a thrift shop earlier in the day. The great poet, by now owner of several pieces of real estate and recent recipient of several highly lucrative awards, just couldn't bring himself to spring for a pair of retail party shoes and limped from his coronation in his socks.

Al, who rode the rails and almost ended up in jail, which would have been death to a free spirit, never left the depression behind. There were many years of

poverty for the Purdys, who wrote their life that way
because of a mutual belief in the importance of poetry
to the growth of a nation. There were times when
they went hungry and other times when they were
only saved from hunger by the kindness of neighbours.

The poet, who achieved fame and a modest for-
tune, stoked the bonfires of vanity, while he and
Eurithe shared the wrong side of the sandwich. There
is nothing glamourous about cold and hunger. Frank
McCourt, the great Irish autobiographer says, "It
makes you mean." McCourt also says the progress of
life is the movement from fear to freedom. This was
the great accomplishment of Al Purdy, the fearful
child who wrote his own ticket to freedom and was
lucky enough to meet a woman who didn't mind
travelling light.

One literal and metaphorical journey was terribly
painful. The same week her husband had an operation
in Victoria for tumours in the lung and around the
heart, their son Jim had a massive heart attack in
Belleville, Ontario, and was on life support. Her heart
stretched over four thousand miles, Eurithe had to
make the only decision a mother can make and left
Al in the hospital for a few days while his own
prognosis set in.

In a hospital room dominated by a huge bouquet
of flowers from Margaret Atwood, he absorbed the
information that birth and copulation, the stage he
assiduously adhered to, were inevitably followed by
death. Just as Atwood's Casa Blanca lilies persisted in

the humid atmosphere of a hospital in summertime, refusing to wilt, the poet refused to go gentle into his goodnight. I, having being left in charge of "discipline," the vitamins and prune juice in Eurithe's regime, was surprised at his vigorous resistance to winding down. At his full four score the poet was mad, mad at the ruthless life cycle and bawling at the wife who temporarily "losted" him just as his mother had when he was three years old.

It was only when I re-read "Homer's Poem" in his *Collected* of 1986 that I understood I was still in the presence of a small child who was afraid of the dark.

> (There's only a hyphen between me and death)
> Listen
> – we are about to be born
> we are soon to become alive
> and fear is always alive
> when death is near.

That last January, his extended family celebrated the eighty-first birthday of a man who would not easily surrender the breath that put its signature on the width and breadth and depth of this country. No wonder he and his contrary bride, who co-signed a precious copy of his latest book, *Pronuncia i nomi/Say the Names*, an Italian selected poems in Italian and English, fought the angel with the big sword. Poetry was at stake. They fought for poetry and the voice sang on.

Never so touchingly as at his party, when he stayed in bed with his sullen intruder until lunch and then rallied to eat from Eurithe's lovely green plates with the younger poets they call family. She sat at one end of the table and he at the other with a handful of fresh birthday poems. Through the meal, he kept looking at her, marvelling at every slight change in expression which proved she was still reacting. "Isn't it wonderful," I reminded him, "that you are having this time to cherish her." " I have no choice," he said. " She controls the oxygen."

Susan, as usual, baked the cake, this time angel food surrounded by green bananas. Everyone laughed. We still are. Otherwise, missing our troublesome boy would be too painful.

GRIEF SITS DOWN

LINDA ROGERS

Every morning now, grief sits down
and drinks her morning coffee with us.
Mostly, we talk about the weather
and the meaning of love,
a word you're still refusing to say.

It has been raining for months,
but today the sky is almost white,
and we can't decide if it's clouds
or dying lessons with all
the unwanted children lined up
in their very best clothes,
getting ready to welcome you there
with the poems and songs you like.

We've all been writing verse,
but our friend, who says she wants
to wear your ashes on her forehead,
but not in the shape of a cross,
insists she was speechless
the day they told her "immortal"
only meant until your last
books are remaindered.

She says the room went white
and she turned her face to the wall.

Who decides this, and who
decides who will be famous and who
will die when the unwanted,
unblessed, unshriven children
all start singing at once?

In the beginning was the word,
which our friend might call "love,"
even though her grieving began
when he told her he loved her less.
Wasn't it love that made her buy
the stained glass window,
a picture of a saint, for her husband
and tape photographs of it to her
breasts when she went to see him
in the visitors room at the white hotel?

Wasn't that what you meant this morning,
when grief sat down and had tea with you
while you remembered the stained glass window
in the house where you and Eurithe
were young and stubborn and blessed,
and how, when the light fell on her face,
even though you couldn't say it,
admit it, you loved her more?

REMEMBERING AL PURDY

SUSAN MUSGRAVE

I met Al Purdy in Mexico – in the Yucatan – in 1972.
He and his wife, Eurithe, were travelling on poet's
wages – staying in cheap motels, shopping for meat
and potatoes in the markets, and cooking on their
own hot-plate. They must have blown up every elec-
trical circuit in the Yucatan. I was all of twenty at the
time; I'd never met anyone like Al, and though he was
one of the most difficult men, in my young, nervous
way, I grew to love him. (How could anyone resist a
poet who takes his own hot-plate to Mexico?) Al was
larger-than-life-size in every way. When he grabbed
you by the arm to talk seriously about the thing he
loved best – poetry – he always left a mark.

I knew his poetry. I knew no subject was too small
or too awkward for Purdy, with his meat and potatoes
small town Canadian sensibility as big as the world's.
His poems had a way of exuding, as Seamus Heaney
has written, "some of the smelly majesty of living".

I also knew the myth, through the poetry others
had written about him, my favourite being "Purdy's
Crocuses" by Tom Wayman. Purdy went to work as
Writer-in-Residence at Loyola in Montreal with a
twelve-pack of beer under each arm, and twice a week
would sit talking to students, reading their poems,

and drinking. He'd recycle his bottles by tossing them out the window.

In the spring, the first thing that appeared out of the melting snow under his office window, was a beer bottle – one, then another, under the whole term's pile of empties was uncovered: "Purdy's crocuses," the students called them. Wayman writes that now whenever he drives across the country (a journey Al and Eurithe made several times each year, from Ameliasburg to the west coast) he doesn't mind so much seeing the dozens of empty beer bottles along the edges of northern Ontario's lonely hardtop, or on Saskatchewan's soft verges.

> What the poet planted in Montreal
> has taken hold, spread coast-to-coast
> like a new brand of cigars or rabbits in Australia:
> slowly the shoulders of the main highways, and the
>   ditches
> along every back road in Canada
> are filling with the brown blooms of Purdy's crocuses.

At one time in his life, Purdy would have been pleased to have the image of a beer bottle evoke his memory. Those were the days when he was known as the hard-drinking, bar-brawling-but-sensitive man; I only really got to know him after he'd stopped drinking, and started listening (a little). And he wasn't easy, as they say in Ireland. Al never could be easy.

For one thing, he would never let you get away with a word used casually or without forethought. If you said "Hello," he would ask if you really meant it. Once, when he came to read his poetry at the Univer-

sity of Waterloo where I was Writer-in-Residence, a
few of us took him to lunch at the Faculty Club. Al
began by picking the tiny shreds of grated carrot out
of his salad. "Carrots," he said, with a certain amount
of horror, as if he had encountered two slugs mating
in his radicchio. And, with even more of a sneer,
"Health food."

When the waiter returned and asked if Al would
care for a bun, I knew the poor boy was in for it.
"Yes," Al said, after considering the matter, deeply
and for a long time, "I *would* care for a bun. I care
for my wife, too. I care for many things. What about
you? What do *you* care for?"

The waiter put the bun on the poet's side plate,
but with excessive hesitation. Purdy was a man who
took words as they were meant to be taken – seriously
– and from that moment on, whenever I was in his
company, I tripped over everything I had to say, and
Purdy took big pleasure in tripping me up every time.

Wherever I have travelled, Al Purdy has been there
first. *And* written poems about it. For instance, when
I reached an age where I began to have a love affair
with Paris, along came Purdy with *To Paris Never
Again*. Purdy doesn't romance the City the way I did
last spring, drinking the best wine in a new good
restaurant every night, leaving Baby's Breath on Os-
car Wilde's grave in Père LaChaisse, taking a boat trip
down the Seine in the rain, being followed through
the narrow streets by a gypsy fire breather who said

he could make the rain stop falling. Purdy, his stom-
ach upset from the drinking water, finds a flea-in-
fested room near the Métro where the noise of the
train shakes him awake all night, sucking him out of
bed as he dreams of Marie Antoinette and Eleanor of
Aquitaine "in a castle the size of Alberta." One of the
things I loved about Al is that he could travel the
world and write poems that never stop reminding us
of his – and our own – Canadianness. Perhaps he was
the quintessential Canadian: a foreigner wherever he
went, and always being mistaken for an American.

His words often take us "somewhere close to
happiness," for holidays in the secret places his poetry
lets us discover inside ourselves. He takes us with him
when he travels back through the centuries into a
marble bath with Agamemnon King of Mycenae,
washing off the dust of travel on his return from Troy,
or climbs a mountain road in Mexico in low gear, or
flies across the prairies where "9/10ths of the landscape is sky / more sunlit heaven than earth," or stands
outside naked in the snow, "in the lazy plunge and
swirl of falling things."

There are few places anyone can go on this planet,
in fact, that Purdy has not been, and written about,
whether it be in the Peruvian Andes, at Machu Pichu,
where he's rejoicing that he's alive in those mountains
– "that life should bring such gifts / and wrap them in
clouds and stars," or at an extended care facility in
Quesnel, interviewing an ancient woman for his B.C.
ghost towns article, or lost in a telephone booth trying
to phone God. Even his poems for the dead speak of

journeys, how he is unable to join his dead friends in that "unknown country," but how he has "invented imaginary souls for them / that kept on living when they died."

"And what am I but what I remember," he asks, in "The Names the Names" (so many dead friends, their names gone into the dark), friends like Tom:

> "years ago when he was especially boring
> and I was taking pride in my bad manners
> I told him so and he said
> "I hope that won't make any difference
> to our friendship"
> which till then I hadn't known existed
> but after that it did . . ."

Our own friendship blossomed (though blossoming is not a word one immediately associates with Al) in 1988 when the Purdys bought a house on the outskirts of Sidney on Vancouver Island. It became clear that my new neighbour would not easily adjust from rural Prince Edward County to living across the road from what I, as a child growing up in the area, had dubbed "the Cold and Windy Beach." I don't remember how it happened, but their house became infested with fleas. Al, his legs covered with red, itchy bites took to dressing in three pairs of wool work socks up to his knees, with his trousers – the kind he had to buy at the Extra Big and Tall Second Hand shop – tucked in at the top. When the fleas moved into the wool, he prepared to repair to Ameliasburg, and leave the west coast to the bug life and other, less sensitive poets.

Marilyn Bowering came up with a solution for him at a party. She said a raccoon rids himself of fleas by taking a piece of grass in his teeth, swimming out into the middle of a lake, then ducking under water with only the tip of the grass sticking out. The fleas would stampede onto the grass, the raccoon would let go of it, and swim back, unencumbered, to shore.

I still have an image of Al, crossing the road to the Cold and Windy Beach, one of his well-masticated wooden matches hanging from the corner of his mouth, power-walking into the cold Pacific. This may be the only time I ever saw him exercise. Al was not big on either health food or being physically fit. His world was of the mind, and here he never lost his grip. Never loosened it for an instant. A week before he died I was sitting at the end of his bed, which felt unusually warm. When I realized I was sitting on his heating pad, I said, "Ohhhhhhhh! I wondered why the bed was so hot!"

"Can't be all that hot, my ass is further up," he gasped, lifting himself so I could see the view.

"Yes," I said, "I see."

"You see?" Al said, making as if to further loosen his dressing gown.

"In a manner of speaking," I said. Even as he lay dying, he wouldn't let me off the hook.

Though our longest sun sets at right declensions and makes but winter arches, it cannot be long before we lie down

in darkness
and have our light in ashes . . . "
(Browne: *Urn Burial*)

In April, the cruelest month of 1999, when Al Purdy was diagnosed as having a tumour on his lung, he didn't refuse to talk about it. Al looked at death the same way he has always looked at life – right between the eyes. ("Nothing is permanent. Our eternal shortness of existence ensures it," he once wrote to me.) When he told me the news he also offered me his last two unopened packages of typing paper, which seemed like a tragically final gesture but also a tragically generous gesture for one who picked up free day-old bread at the Salvation Army and confessed to using bleach to remove the postage marks on stamps. Of the paper, he said, "I won't be needing it." (When I insisted he might still have reams to write before he slept, Eurithe took one of the packages back, but I kept the other.)

All of us, his friends, tried to be brave. Some dedicated poems to him, some sent flowers. Patrick Lane obsessively baked bread – more than Al could eat in a lifetime. "Why don't you hurry up and die so I can stop baking!" Patrick demanded, at the last dinner party where the six of us were together. My husband cut wood on Al and Eurithe's beach during the storms that last spring, to keep our home fires burning.

Each time I visited their house, Al asked me if, when the time came, I would like some of his ashes.

Each time, I squirmed, it being hard to imagine
someone who takes up the enormous psychic and
physical space Al does in the world, having his light
in ashes.

Finally, I responded the only way I could, by
writing a poem – "32 Uses for Al Purdy's Ashes" –
more of a tribute to his poetry, than a poem about
mortality. The poem begins:

> Smuggle them to Paris and fling them
> into the Seine. P.S. He was wrong
> when he wrote, "To Paris Never Again"

and goes on to suggest various other ways of employ-
ing his mortal remains: putting them in an egg-timer
so he could go on being useful; sprinkling them, when
you're stuck in deep snow, under your bald tires for
traction; declaring them culturally modified property
and having them preserved for posterity in the Museum of Modern Man, and, as Purdy would be the
first to add, Modern Wife; placing them beside your
bed where they can watch you make love, vulgarly
and immensely, in the little time left.

Al seemed pleased with the poem, though he grew
less enthused with it the closer he came to death. The
day before he died he told me the best lines in my
poem were his, and demanded 50% of any money I
made, in perpetuity. He was right, of course. The best
lines are always his. And, as always, he got there first.

> – and now far into old age
> with its inevitable conclusion

I am deeply troubled
a profound literary sadness
of knowing I am using death
too much in poems
but turn about
is fair play I guess and
I expect to have it use me
soon for its own purposes
whatever those might be
and it won't be for poems.

One day when I reach that "unknown country" my-self, there is one thing I'll know: Al Purdy will have been there and written a poem about it, before moving on to wherever it is we go.

THIRTY TWO USES FOR AL PURDY'S ASHES

SUSAN MUSGRAVE

Smuggle them to Paris and fling them
into the Seine. P.S. He was wrong
when he wrote, "To Paris Never Again"

Put them in an egg-timer – that way
he can go on being useful, at least
for three minutes at a time
(pulverize him first, in a blender)

Like his no good '48 Pontiac
refusing to turn over in below zero weather,
let the wreckers haul his ashes away

Or stash them in the trunk of your car:
when you're stuck in deep snow sprinkle them
under your bald tires for traction

Mix them with twenty tons of concrete,
like Lawrence at Taos, erect
a permanent monument to his banned
poetry in Fenelon Falls

Shout "these ashes oughta be worth some beer!"

in the tavern at the Quinte Hotel, and wait
for a bottomless glass with yellow flowers in it
to appear

Mix one part ashes to three parts
homemade beer in a crock under the table,
stir with a broom, and consume
in excessive moderation

Fertilize the dwarf trees at the Arctic Circle
so that one day they might grow to be
as tall as he, always the first
to know when it was raining

Scatter them at Roblin's Mills
to shimmer among the pollen
or out over Roblin Lake
where the great *boing* they make
will arouse summer cottagers

Place them beside your bed where they can
watch you make love, vulgarly
and immensely, in the little time left
Declare them an aphrodisiac, more potent
than the gallbladder of a bear
with none of the side-effects of Viagra

Stitch them in the hem of your summer dress
where his weight will keep it
from flying up in the wind, exposing
everything: he would like that

Let them harden, the way the heart must harden
as the might lessens, then lob them
at the slimy, drivelling, snivelling,
palsied, pulseless lot of critics who ever uttered
a single derogatory phrase in anti-praise
of his poetry

Award them the Nobel Prize
for humility

Administer them as a dietary supplement
to existential Eskimo dogs with a preference
for violet toilet paper and violent
appetites for human excrement: dogs
that made him pray daily
for constipation in Pangnirtung

Bequeath them to Margaret Atwood,
casually inserted between the covers
of Wm Barrett's *Irrational Man*

Lose them where the ghosts of his Cariboo
horses graze on, when you stop to buy oranges
from the corner grocer at 100 Mile House

Distribute them from a hang-glider
over the Galapagos Islands
where blue-footed boobies will shield him
from over-exposure to ultraviolet rays

Offer them as a tip to the shoeshine boys
on the Avenida Juarez, all twenty of them

who once shined his shoes for one peso
and 20 centavos – 9 and a half cents –
years ago when 9 and a half cents
was worth twice that amount

Encapsulate them in the ruins of Quintana Roo
under the green eyes of quetzals, Tulum parrots,
and the blue, unappeasable sky –
that 600 years later they may still be warm
Declare them culturally modified property
and have them preserved for posterity
in the Museum of Modern Man, and, as
he would be the first to add, Modern Wife

As a last resort auction them off
to the highest bidder, the archives
at Queens or Cornell where
Auden's tarry lungs wheeze on
next to the decomposed kidneys of Dylan Thomas;
this will ensure Al's survival in Academia, also

But on no account cast his ashes to the wind:
they will blow back in your face as if to say
he is, in some form, poetic or other, here
to stay, with sestinas still to write
and articles to rewrite
for *The Imperial Oil Review*

No, give these mortal remains away
that they be used as a mojo to end the dirty
cleansing in Kosovo, taken as a cure
for depression in Namu, B.C., for defeat

in the country north of Belleville, for poverty
hopping a boxcar west out of Winnipeg
all the way to Vancouver, for heroin addiction
in Vancouver; a cure for loneliness
in North Saanich, for love in Oaxaca,
courtship in Cuernavaca, adultery
in Ameliasburg, the one sure cure
for extremely deep hopelessness
in the Eternal City, for death, everywhere,
pressed in a letter sent whispering to you.

THE DECLINING DAYS OF AL PURDY

CATHERINE PORTER

At the height of the politically correct 1990s, Purdy was anything but . . . He scraped himself down with the razor of honesty – beneath the veneer of humour was all the awkwardness, fear, contempt, shame. He once wrote that poetry was a 'condition for living' for him, and he approached it like he did bar brawls, directly, without blinking, never backing down.

It wasn't until last September that I discovered Al Purdy had died. I'd spent the year in India and returned to my parents' home to find a newspaper article dutifully clipped and left on my childhood desk titled: "One of the Country's Great Poets, Al Purdy, has died of cancer." It was dated April 24, 2000.

I was bewildered, as if I had expected to feel the ground shift as far away as the Himalayas when Purdy pulled both thumbs from the stony earth of the Canadian shield. It seemed too much like a good Purdy prank to be true – convincing the country he had passed away and then stowing away in his workroom to grimace and chuckle over the obituaries. I half expected to find an envelope in the same pile addressed with his trademark wonkily typed letters, containing a note that started with "haw haw."

Of course, there was no new letter. The last I received from him was dated January 27, 1999 – a few months before he went in for an operation to clean out the cancer in his lungs. He said he hadn't written many poems over the past year, which by his own definition meant he wasn't truly living. The letter was longer than most of his earlier ones, and typed on clean white paper, with no signs of Liquid Paper or old letterhead with "New College" or "Norithan Inc." he had collected over the years. (I always put Purdy's eclectic stationery down to his earlier poverty, when he couldn't afford paper to write on and was reduced to eating roadkill donated by the neighbours. In an earlier letter, he relayed a story about returning home from a poetry reading in the early 1960s and noticing a bulk of paper in a garbage can. After stuffing it into his suitcase, the zipper split and spilled his recent claim over the floor of the Kingston Bus Terminal. "Would be embarrassing if I were easily embarrassed," he wrote.)

But the voice it contained was typically Al – both practical and whimsical, mildly flirtatious and faintly derisive, at once offering advice and then discrediting it by saying "you'll have to decide for yourself because everyone's different."

I first met Purdy in the summer of 1996, while doing research for the publisher Jack McClelland's memoir. Before dialling the poet's number in Ameliasburg, I nervously set my empty diary before me. I hoped he could squeeze me into his busy schedule for a couple of hours sometime over the next two months. The voice that answered the phone was hollow and rusty and pungent; a moosecall in rutting season. It was Purdy. After he grumbled that his relationship with McClelland was inconsequential, he complied: "Sure, why don't you come over right now?"

I couldn't. I was in Toronto – a two-hour drive away.

"How 'bout tomorrow then?" he said. We settled on the following week. I was then, and probably still am, a sheltered, affluent, squeaky-clean twenty-something woman with too much education. And I was scared to death by my desire to write.

Purdy was a 76-year-old high-school dropout who had rode the rails across the country during the Depression, taken up menial jobs at mattress factories to support his family (barely) and his own passion, and shown the courage to publish his own first volume of poetry himself in 1944. Since then, he had written more than thirty books of poetry and prose, won two Governor General's Awards and been honoured with the Order of Canada.

I tried to calm my nervousness by preparing – going over university class notes, rereading many of his poems, studying his autobiography *Reaching for the Beaufort Sea* and driving to Hamilton to dig through the box of correspondence between him and McClelland housed in the McMaster University library.

What I found was unsettling. At the height of the politically correct 1990s, Purdy was anything but.

The frankness he used to celebrate the country often turned inward to more delicate issues. He scraped himself down with the razor of honesty – beneath the veneer of humour was all the awkwardness, fear, contempt, shame. He once wrote that poetry was a "condition of living" for him, and he approached it like he did bar brawls, directly, without blinking, never backing down. He spoke about all these things plainly, without pretence. Sometimes it came off as jocular – the pissing behind the house, the "sensitive man" jumping into a bar brawl, the hobo life. But even then it was searingly human.

In "On Being Human," he recounts visiting his dying mother in the hospital and "something in my face made her say /'I thought you'd feel terrible'/ and she meant that I'd be devastated / by what had happened to her / – I wasn't feeling anything very much / at the time and I guess it showed . . . and I am still ashamed / and I am still alive."

He was like the uncouth relative who always said the unspeakable at a family gathering. It wasn't only in his poetry. Going through his letters, I found he could be as blunt as a sledgehammer. It separated him from most writers who were fawning in their letters to their publisher.

I worried he'd find my questions too simple and peel back my insecurities like the skin of an onion. That day I drove through Belleville to Ameliasburg, past Purdy lane and the library that has since been named after him, and down to Roblin Lake. I thought I would be able to identify the Purdys' A-frame structure from miles away, having built it in my mind while reading all the poems like "An Arrogance" and "House Guest" – up there with him and Milton Acorn, "working with saw and hammer at the house all winter afternoon/disagreeing about how to pound nails . . . Every morning I'd get up and say 'Look at the nails – / you snored them out half an inch in the night.' "

But, it was obstructed from the road, and I ended up having to ask directions from the bemused neighbour next door. His life-long partner and wife, Eurithe, opened the door and welcomed me in. The house was tidier and more polished than I thought it would be.

Purdy appeared from his study, an apparition, towering at 6-foot-3, with big hands and an awkward stance. He wore large, tinted glasses, and his white hair fell off the bald rim of his head like the wild last few tufts of a dandelion. He looked every bit his voice.

We were steered to a table overlooking the lake, where he slumped back in his chair, a bored teenager, rocking it up on its hind legs, his own legs sprawled out before him. Some questions disinterested him and were shrugged off with a mere "no" or "I don't remember." The others – the ones he wanted to talk about – he got to long before I asked.

He recounted stories of publicity stunts, meetings at bars and the heated arguments over a proposed book he was to produce with artist Harold Town. Purdy once wrote to Margaret Laurence "probably anything I ever thought was important got into a poem sooner or later," and many of his anecdotes rang familiar.

He crooned over McClelland's former editors, the first of whom was my mother. "You do look like your mother. Almost as pretty as she was."

And he ended the interview with a final jab at Town, with whom there had never been a reconciliation: "Town was such a nasty piece of work. Just because he's dead doesn't mean he was sweet."

Afterward, he took me on a tour, first pointing to the beams he had to redo because "Acorn hammered them in crooked." There on the roof was the place from which he had fallen and frozen in a poem I had found in the boxes at McMaster titled Icarus: "What do you think about / in those last few seconds / when you know you are going to die."

It all had a comforting effect. I felt like I had stepped into one of his poems, and he allowed me to revel in places as they overlapped with my own mental images of them. It occurred to me that since Purdy wrote about himself so frankly, I felt almost maternal toward him, like I had watched him grow up. I had overseen his lonely childhood, his voyages to South America and the Arctic, chuckled at his labour-intensive attempts to make wild-grape wine, witnessed his first romantic fumblings and the development of his relationship with Eurithe, even their dramatic quarrels, and most recently sympathized with him over the death of his friends.

All this made me drunk with enthusiasm. Having

just returned from South America, I wanted to compare notes. I told him I had also made it up "the neighbouring / mountain Birney once climbed / completely mist-obscured" at Machu Picchu, and the next week included a photo of me there with my thank-you letter.

I was surprised to get a reply: "I've taped your picture up on my wall, thinking that triumphant grin is a tonic I need in my work room."

I skipped to the subway that day. I wrote him back immediately and a correspondence was struck that would continue over the next four years, with me sending letters off to Ameliasburg in the summer and to the Purdys' winter home in Sydney, British Columbia, and in turn finding his replies in the letter box of my apartment in Toronto and later Vancouver.

They were riddled with Purdy-esque vernacular like "helluva" and "I dunno," and typos that from time to time seemed too devious to be accidental. In one letter, he describes the salmon creek outside his window where "a family of fucks is often in residence, sometimes mallards."

But they weren't the letters of a mentor to an aspiring writer. Were they letters from "an old man in his declining days" who was flattered by the attention of a young woman? In part, I'm sure.

Purdy was a renowned letter-writer, though. It was his way of both workshopping his poems and creating a community. His correspondence with Margaret Laurence, George Woodcock and American writer Charles Bukowski have been published in three thick volumes. He also took many young poets under his wing. Maybe he had more faith in my writing ability than I did. As he says in *Reaching for the Beaufort Sea*: "I'm forced to confess, I don't know why friendship exists, just pleased that it does."

Between letters, I met him at a number of his readings. But it wasn't until the spring of 1998 that I made it out to Sydney to visit him again. It was raining when I pulled up to their little white house that looked onto the Georgia Strait. This time, he opened the door, hands on hips. Almost immediately, he took me down to his basement workroom. Only one small window spilled in light on his cramped wooden desk. Across the room was a small labyrinth of shelves, all stacked with books, and behind the desk a small glass case where he kept his more precious titles.

His excitement was contagious. He was like a kid in an amusement park, pulling out one treasure or another to show me: a first edition Yeats; a signed copy of poems by Wallace Stevens; the two original letters by D. H. Lawrence whom he considered his mentor.

After a half-hour, he announced we should go upstairs, where we ate fish and talked about our travels across the country. At one point, he rolled up his pant legs to show me how dead nerve endings had made his calves go bald. "Ungh," he honked. "I'm getting old."

But nothing about him seemed old then. It's been a year now since he died and I am only just coming to accept there won't be any more of his letters arriving. His voice is now my mind's Tourette's syndrome, croaking wry thoughts I would never have the gumption to say. And sometimes when I spring without notice into a skip down the street before the amused eyes of strangers, I can hear him cackling. I wonder what his last thoughts before dying were. Like his Icarus though, I know he looked it straight in the eyes without blinking.

BIBLIOGRAPHY

POETRY

The Enchanted Echo, 1944
Pressed on Sand, 1955
Emu, Remember! 1956
The Crafte So Long to Lerne, 1959
The Blur in Between: Poems 1960-61, 1962
Poems for All the Annettes, 1962
The Cariboo Horses, 1965
North of Summer: Poems from Baffin Island, 1967
Wild Grape Wine, 1968
Love in a Burning Building, 1970
The Quest for Ouzo, 1971
Hiroshima Poems, 1972
Selected Poems, 1972
On the Bearpaw Sea, 1973
Sex and Death, 1973
In Search of Owen Roblin, 1974
The Poems of Al Purdy: A New Canadian Library Selection, 1976
Sundance at Dusk, 1976
A Handful of Earth, 1977
At Marsport Drugstore, 1977
Moths in the Iron Curtain, 1977
No Second Spring, 1977
Being Alive: Poems 1958-78, 1978
The Stone Bird, 1981
Birdwatching at the Equator: The Galapagos Islands, 1982
Bursting into Song: An Al Purdy Omnibus, 1982
Piling Blood, 1984
The Collected Poems of Al Purdy, 1986
The Woman on the Shore, 1990
Naked with Summer in Your Mouth, 1994
Rooms for Rent in the Outer Planets, 1996
To Paris Never Again, 1997
In Mexico (Deluxe Limited Edition with Alan Stein, illus.), 1997

The Man Who Outlived Himself, with Doug Beardsley, 1999
Pronuncia i nomi/ Say the Names (Italian-English collection), 1999
Home Country (Deluxe Limited Edition with Alan Stein, illus.), 2000
Beyond Remembering: The Collected Poems of Al Purdy, 2000

OTHER

No Other Country, prose, 1977
The Bukowsky/Purdy Letters, 1964-1974: A decade of dialogue with Charles Bukowski, 1983
Morning and It's Summer: A memoir, 1983
The George Woodcock/Al Purdy Letters, edited by George Gault, 1987
A Splinter in the Heart, novel, 1990
Cougar Hunter, essay on Roderick Haig-Brown, 1993
Margaret Laurence/Al Purdy: A Friendship in Letters, 1993
Reaching for the Beaufort Sea: An Autobiography, 1993
Starting from Ameliasburg: The Collected Prose of Al Purdy, 1995
No One Else Is Lawrence!, with Doug Beardsley, 1998

EDITOR

The New Romans: Candid Canadian Opinions of the US, 1968
Fifteen Winds: A Selection of Modern Canadian Poems, 1969
Milton Acorn: I've Tasted My Blood, Poems 1956-68 (1969)
Storm Warning: The New Canadian Poets, 1971
Storm Warning 2: The New Canadian Poets, 1976
Andrew Suknaski, Wood Mountain Poems, 1976

CASSETTE TAPE

The Collected Poems, 1986

COMPACT DISC

Necropsy of Love, 1999